Diasporas in the Contemporary World

DIASPORAS IN THE CONTEMPORARY WORLD

Milton J. Esman

polity

First published in 2009 by Polity Press

Polity Press
65 Bridge Street
Cambridge CB2 1UR, UK

Polity Press
350 Main Street
Malden, MA 02148, USA

ISBN-13: 978-0-7456-4496-7
ISBN-13: 978-0-7456-4497-4 (pb)

A catalogue record for this book is available from the British
Library.

Typeset in 11 on 13pt Berling Roman
by Servis Filmsetting Ltd, Stockport, Cheshire
Printed and bound by MPG Books Group, UK

For further information on Polity, visit our website:
www.politybooks.com

Contents

Introduction

During October 2005 and again in October 2006 and November 2007, the north African ghettos in the suburbs surrounding Paris and other French cities erupted in riots that inflicted very heavy damage on police officers and on the property of every visible institution representing the French state. These riots were judged by the police to constitute urban guerilla warfare. In 2005 they persisted for four weeks before they were finally brought under control. They demonstrated the rage and the hostility of French-born members of France's large Muslim north African diaspora toward the symbols of the French state and French society. France, they claim, disrespects them and their culture, systematically discriminates against them, and condemns them to unemployment or to menial, dead-end jobs. Already they number 8 percent of France's population and their high birth rate guarantees that that proportion will increase. As France rejects them, so they reject France. They expect to remain in France, but never to become French.

Less dramatically, Muslim Turks in Germany and Switzerland, Pakistanis in Britain, and similar diasporas in Denmark and Spain, the Netherlands and Austria decline to accept citizenship, even when it is available. In a process of mutual revulsion, most Europeans are reluctant to accept them as fellow countrymen. Many are suspected as security risks, as harboring terrorists. Consequently, immigration and the fate of these diasporas have become the principal emotionally charged issues on the agendas of Europe's governments. Late in 2007, the plans of a group of wealthy Muslims to construct in London's East End the largest mosque in Europe, exceeding in size St Paul's cathedral, evoked passionate opposition throughout Britain.[1]

Must Europeans contemplate the specter of permanent parallel societies, hostile diasporas, in their homelands?

The United States has been more fortunate. It is rapidly absorbing into its mainstream culture and society the largest wave of immigration in its history. These new diasporas, Hispanic and Asian, had long suffered discrimination and exclusion prior to the Civil Rights revolution of the 1960s. Though racism has not lost its sting and immigration, especially illegal immigration, remains a contentious issue in American politics, the American opportunity structure is steadily assimilating the children of its Latino and Asian diasporas into its mainstream economy, polity, and society.

Diasporas are a consequential presence in Europe and America. But what explains the differences in their reception and their response?

1
What are diasporas, why do they matter?

Diasporas are the consequence of transnational migration. Throughout human history, people singly, more often in groups, have moved across international borders. In prehistoric biblical lore, the patriarch, Jacob, led his extended family and kinfolk and their flocks from drought-stricken Canaan to Egypt, where food and fodder were plentiful. Their diaspora multiplied, was enslaved by Egypt's rulers, and subsequently led out of bondage to freedom, crossing international borders until they reached their promised land.[1]

Diasporas arrive as conquerors and settlers, like Spaniards in the Americas and Saxons and their successors, the Normans in Britain; as refugees escaping war or persecution, like Huguenots in seventeenth-century South Africa and Iraqi Sunni in contemporary Sweden; as peasants fleeing drought, famine, or overpopulation, like nineteenth-century Irish and Mexicans in twenty-first-century America; as unemployed laborers, like Turks and north Africans in contemporary Europe; as skilled workers or highly educated professionals, like contemporary Asians in Silicon Valley and Vancouver; or as merchants seeking new products to trade or new markets to exploit, like Indian traders in east Africa and Lebanese in west Africa. Migrants usually move voluntarily, but some are coerced, like Africans transported in chains to be slave laborers in the Americas.

Never have there been so many transnational migrants as during the current era. According to United Nations estimates, in 2005 as many as 228 million people lived outside their country of birth, comprising 3 percent of world population.[2] With globalization the numbers continue to grow. Fast, cheap, safe, and reliable airline transportation has facilitated international travel, while instantaneous, inexpensive communications technologies, telephone and e-mail, enable migrants to keep closely in touch with families and friends in their former homeland. The majority of migrants move from low-income to the rich, industrialized countries where they can often multiply their previous incomes by a factor of 5. A minority, however, move to middle-income countries, such as Malaysia, Libya, and Chile, or even to low-income countries such as Nigeria and India where they take advantage of job opportunities that were unavailable in their homelands.

Despite the popular impression that transnational migrants are among the poorest of the poor in their countries of origin, this proves to be seldom the case. An important reason is that the process of migration usually requires money, to cover the costs of necessary transportation and subsistence while en route, the payment of exit and entrance visas and of bribes to officials and facilitators when this is necessary, and similar expenses. The required funds may be provided as gifts or as loans from family members and friends. Altogether, these may add up to substantial amounts beyond the capacity of the very poor.

Many migrants originally regard themselves as sojourners who have left their homeland temporarily, intending eventually to return, and are so regarded by officials and the public in their host country. As many as a third do eventually return to their homelands. Yet, the great majority, having rebuilt their lives in their host country, choose, when this is possible, to remain, as do their locally born and locally educated children. They form communities, hoping to retain their inherited culture and to reproduce, as much as possible, the familiar environment of their former homeland. In residential enclaves in urban areas, they establish institutions to serve their distinctive religious, cultural, social, informational, entertainment, and economic needs and to relate to the society and to officialdom in their host country. These communities in host countries constitute the diaspora from their country of origin.

Members of the immigrant generation, but decreasingly of succeeding generations, tend to lead transnational existences, economically and occupationally in their host country, but socially and culturally still in the old country. At home and in their neighborhood they communicate in their native language. They follow athletic and political events in the old country, they listen to radio broadcasts and read publications from their homeland or news and entertainment broadcast and published locally in their maternal language. They remit funds to help family members they have left behind; they contribute funds to political movements that they favor in their homeland, and support candidates for public office. In many cases as dual citizens, they are permitted to vote in elections in their former homeland, as well as in their adopted country. They call upon their homeland for cultural reinforcement, usually in the form of teachers and religious leaders, to help maintain their ancestral culture; governments and associations in the homeland eagerly provide them. They keep in touch with relatives and friends who have formed similar diaspora communities in other countries and in other cities in their host country, and provide help when this is needed.

The homeland which they continue to regard with affection is usually the country from which they emigrated, more specifically, the village or province they have left behind and where their family, relatives, and the burial sites of their forebears remain. In a few cases, however, the "homeland" is an ideological construct, the product of collective memory or myth. Italians, Chinese, Mexicans in their diasporas can relate to particular settlements and a real homeland. But Jews, for millennia, yearned for Jerusalem as the lost homeland they had never seen, but could only visualize in their imagination. As they moved from eastern Europe to the

United States, their nostalgia was not for Poland or Rumania, where they had suffered discrimination and exclusion, but for their mythologized Jerusalem. Even after Israel became a twentieth-century reality, most diaspora Jews could treat it as their idealized homeland, even though neither they nor their ancestors had ever experienced it.

While they remember their homeland, their daily existence must focus on their host country. It is there that they find jobs, open businesses, and are exposed to the local popular culture and political events through the local mass media. These require some familiarity and fluency with the mainstream language. They are drawn into athletic events and political contests, increasing their feeling of belonging to the host nation. If they encounter exclusion or discrimination, they may try even harder to win acceptance. When these efforts fail, they may cease trying and focus their energies on the institutions of the diaspora. They may even respond to rejection by rejection. Where the opportunity structure permits, they may qualify for citizenship. The arrival of children increases their incentive to feel at home in their adopted country, since the children may be birthright citizens and regard the local language and culture as their own. But while members of the diaspora community adapt to the environment around them, they still maintain transnational sentimental and material links with their former homeland.

On a global scale, annual remittances from diasporas to their home countries exceeded $251 billion in 2007, more than double total foreign aid flows to less developed countries.[3] To illustrate the economic importance of diasporas to their home country: funds remitted from overseas to family members in the Philippines in 2005 exceeded a billion US dollars a month, more than 10 percent of national GNP.[4] Diasporas may be equally important to the economies of their host countries. Among fruit and vegetable growers in California, labor from the Mexican diaspora is indispensable to the prosperity of that important industry. Similar dependence on the diaspora's economic contribution can be replicated in numerous industries throughout North America,

Europe, and the Middle East where local labor is unavailable or unwilling to perform hard, dirty, monotonous, sometimes dangerous tasks at substandard wages. Diasporas have become essential to the smooth functioning of the economies of many advanced industrial countries.

Outgoing members of the diaspora soon learn and use the local language, and participate in mainstream educational, political, and economic institutions. They may, where this is possible, serve in the national armed forces, campaign in elections, and hold public office. They may maintain a dual or hybrid identity, summoning the one or the other as different situations require. In the morning they may participate in a national independence day celebration in their host country, while in the afternoon of the same day they remit funds to a political movement and applaud the success of a soccer team from their former homeland. Because of their bi-national identities and associations, they are vulnerable to the charge of "dual loyalty" by nativists in their host country.

Nativists in all host countries nourish their hostility to immigrants, especially to "visible" immigrants of different races and their exotic cultures. Such immigrants, they charge, bring crime and disease into their country; they simply do not belong, can never be integrated into the national political and social community. Assuming their labor is needed, they can be admitted only for short stays, then required to leave. They may be harassed by police and by young nativist toughs and suffer discrimination in all the institutions of their host country. From Japan to Germany, from France to the United States, politicians attempt to build constituencies by exploiting public hostility to immigrants, especially to those who have entered the country and remain illegally. In May 2007, France elected a President who had talked tough about north African immigrants, referring to them as "scum." Nativists and their sympathizers clash with proponents of human rights, who urge the necessity of humane treatment of immigrants, of welcoming them into mainstream institutions on a non-discriminatory basis, and of recognizing the benefits to the nation of social and ethnic diversity.

While some countries, among them the United States, encourage members of diasporas to integrate into the mainstream, others, including the Persian Gulf petroleum emirates, strictly forbid it, keeping migrants at arm's length and requiring them to return to their homelands when their labor contracts expire. Some diaspora communities insist on maintaining their distinctive identity and resist acculturation and assimilation into the local mainstream. Examples are Amish and Hasidic Jews in the United States, Asians in east Africa, and Lebanese in west Africa.

The presence of diasporas generates ethnic conflict. It may be contained and resolved within established political institutions, but it sometimes turns violent. Foreign communities in their midst speaking exotic languages, dressing strangely, practicing unfamiliar customs – these create suspicions: what are these foreigners doing in our country? Are they or might they become security risks? Are they or will they become criminals, spread diseases, or overwhelm our schools and abuse our welfare services? Then come demands from spokespersons for the diaspora for special treatment: bilingual education, time off for religious rites and festivals, provisions for the maintenance of their separate culture, nondiscriminatory access to higher education and employment. Every one of these issues can produce tensions and conflicts with native groups that perceive their neighborhoods, jobs or national culture to be threatened by the aggressive encroachment of unwanted foreigners.

Diasporas have become important non-state actors in international affairs – a reality that we explore in chapter 5. They may support or oppose the government of their home country, morally, financially, and as suppliers of weapons and even personnel to the faction they favor. They may support their homeland government when it is engaged in warfare and boycott the products of its enemies. In peacetime, as we have indicated, their financial remittances can constitute an important fillip to the external accounts of their former homeland. Homelands and host governments as well attempt to call upon diaspora communities to support their strategic objectives. And diasporas may request their host governments or their homelands to intervene on their behalf. In the 1970s the Jewish diaspora in the United States successfully urged its government to demand as a matter of human rights that the reluctant Soviet regime allow dissident Jews, "refuseniks," to emigrate. Overseas Chinese financed the nationalist movement that overthrew the Imperial Ch'ing regime in 1911 and established the new nationalist government; they boycotted the manufactured products of the Japanese invaders of their homeland in the 1930s; in the 1990s they became the largest providers of foreign capital and technologies that accelerated the industrial modernization and spectacular economic growth of the post-Maoist Chinese economy.

Diasporas thus function in a trilateral set of relationships that involve 1) their country of origin, the homeland, its government, political movements, mass media sources of information, their extended family and friends; 2) their host country, its government, and the economic, political, educational, and informational institutions that affect the survival, well-being, and adaptation of the diaspora to its new and often less-than-friendly environment; and 3) the diaspora itself and its many linkages with the homeland, host country, and segments of the diaspora in other countries and in other cities in its host country. Diasporas, moreover, tend to be riven by internal factions that pull in different directions. Thus, efforts to map the diaspora's complex network of linkages confound attempts to make general statements about the behavior or the fate of diaspora communities. Nor is it helpful to treat diasporas as mere social constructs, products of inquiring minds, transient collections of individuals rather then communities.[5] I find it more useful to regard them as real social structures, not imagined communities, produced by the movement of men and women across international borders and the clustering together in separate residential enclaves of persons of similar ethnic provenance for mutual protection, assistance, and fellowship.

Diasporas consist of the original immigrant generation plus their progeny, as long as they choose to or are forced to remain a separate community. If they encounter a relatively open society, such as Australia, that encourages acculturation and eventual assimilation; and unless the diaspora community is replenished by streams of fresh arrivals, it may, within a few generations, gradually be absorbed through accultura- tion and intermarriage into the host society and disappear as a recognizable entity. Its former residential enclaves atrophy, as do its institutions that are no longer sustained by descend- ents of the earlier generations. Some individuals who have integrated into the mainstream may continue, through nos- talgia, affection for grandparents, or respect for traditions, to identify with and continue to support the enfeebled institu- tions of their ethnic heritage, though these no longer influence their day-to-day lifestyle. Diasporas, following this scenario, may indeed disappear from history. Examples are the Russian diaspora in France, and the Dutch and Swedish diasporas in the United States. With intermarriage now exceeding 50 percent, the Japanese diaspora in the US is in the process of withering. Diasporas that are reinforced by a separate religious tradition are likely to prove more long- lasting, even when their members have been fully acculturated to the local mainstream and participate actively in main- stream institutions. Examples are Armenians in France, Jews in Britain, and Greeks in the United States.

Where the local society is hostile to ethnic diversity and resistant to accepting members of a diaspora that has estab- lished a community in its midst, that diaspora is likely to respond to rejection and discrimination by falling back on its institutions and traditions and by rejecting, in turn, well- meaning overtures by representatives of the host society. It may demand a multicultural policy by the host government or recognition of permanent separate status and minority group rights, similar to those accorded to Malaysia's Chinese. Individuals may, however, find opportunities to gain access to educational institutions or to employment or business niches in the local economy. These signal success and enable them to keep one foot in mainstream society, the other foot in the diaspora.

Generally, exclusion and discrimination create grievances that result in disaffected communities that are permanently present in the host country. Their youthful, locally born and locally educated members may respond to their frustrations by socially delinquent and criminal behavior and violence, leading even to insurrection. During the 1970s and 1980s, there were violent outbreaks in several British cities in Greater London and the Midlands by young members of the Afro-Caribbean diaspora. They were protesting flagrant discrimination in employment and housing, and abusive treatment by government agencies, notably the police. In response, the government instituted programs to accommodate these demands. As a result, violent incidents between whites and blacks, including government agencies and the police, have virtually ceased. As an unanticipated consequence of this success, Pakistani immigrants have more recently complained that government agencies discriminate against them in favor of Afro-Caribbeans. While affirmative action for black businesspeople is no longer protested by whites, it is perceived by Pakistani shopkeepers as discrimination against them. Tensions between Afro-Caribbean and south Asian gangs have increased, including two nights of violent encounters in Birmingham in October 2005.[6] As two diaspora communities compete for the same turf and economic opportunities, their young male members may clash violently.

Within the host country, the benefits and costs resulting from labor diasporas are distributed unequally by economic class. The upper and middle classes generally benefit from immigrant labor. They experience no competition from immigrants for housing or jobs, but benefit from an abundant supply of cheap, docile, and willing household help and gardeners; as employers, they have a pool of hard-working, uncomplaining manpower willing to work for wages and under conditions in slaughterhouses and construction sites and on farms that would not be tolerated by members of the native workforce. Immigrant labor, including illegals, makes possible the reliable, year-round supply of inexpensive fruit and vegetables to middle-class consumers in the United

States and Canada. Less skilled native workers, on the other hand, experience labor diasporas as competitors for jobs, undercutting wage rates and violating labor standards; and as competitors for affordable housing, raising rents and forcing native workers and their families to abandon neighborhoods that they had long called home.

Economic costs and benefits are not the only determinants of native attitudes toward immigrants. Middle-class individuals may be upset by the foreign speech that they encounter on the streets of their cities and the foreign language signs that appear on store fronts. Fear that their nation is being overwhelmed by a flood of undesirable, often dark-skinned foreigners who abuse its welfare programs and bring crime and disease to their community is more a middle-class than a working-class reaction to visible foreigners. Middle-class concerns are more likely to be highlighted politically than those of the working classes. In the United States, for example, middle-class outrage about "amnesty" for undocumented law breakers has yielded more political traction than working-class concerns about immigrants threatening their livelihoods and "stealing" their jobs.

In chapter 2, we disaggregate diasporas into several classes that facilitate analysis and understanding.

2
Definition and classes of diasporas

In his 1997 volume, Robin Cohen set forth what he believes to be the common features of diasporas:[1]

1. dispersal from an original homeland, often traumatically, to two or more foreign regions;
2. alternatively, the expansion from a homeland in search of work, in pursuit of trade, or to further colonial ambitions;
3. a collective memory and myth about the homeland, including its location, history, and achievements;
4. an idealization of the putative ancestral home and a collective commitment to its maintenance, restoration, safety, and prosperity, even to its creation;
5. the development of a return movement that gains collective approbation;
6. a strong ethnic group consciousness sustained over a long time and based on a sense of distinctiveness, a common history, and the belief in a common fate;
7. a troubled relationship with host societies, suggesting a lack of acceptance at the least or the possibility that another calamity might befall the group;
8. a sense of empathy and solidarity with co-ethnic members in other countries of settlement; and

9. the possibility of a distinctive, creative, enriching life in host countries with a tolerance for pluralism.

Except for item 2, which fits awkwardly into this listing, these listed features encompass the classical concept of diasporas, modeled on the Jewish experience. Item 2, the "alternative" definition, is a concession to the more modern usage of the term that covers *any transnational migrant community that maintains material or sentimental attachments to its country of origin (its home country), while adapting to the limitations and opportunities in its country of settlement (its host country)*. Departure from its homeland need not have been violent or "traumatic" (item 1), the home country need not be "idealized" (item 4) and members of the diaspora need not conceive or yearn for a return movement (item 5).[2] While they maintain linkages with their former homeland, their principal energies and resources are devoted to adapting to the day-to-day opportunities and limitations they experience in their host country.

Departures from the classical concept of diaspora and acceptance of the expanded, modern definition have become routine usage in public discourse and among contemporary scholars.[3] It was employed by McCaffrey in 1976 in his treatment of the Irish diaspora; enunciated by Sheffer and his associates in 1986; followed by Van Hear who applied it to Mexicans in the United States; by Munz and Ohliger who applied it to migrants from the defunct Soviet Union, including Russians in Israel; and by the authors in the Routledge series who applied it to the contemporary Sikh, the Italian, the Israeli, the Hindu and the Ukrainian diasporas. All of them transcend the classical concept and conform to the modern usage of the term: to repeat, a migrant community that maintains material or sentimental linkages with its home country, while adapting to the environment and institutions of its host country.[4] This is the concept and definition of diasporas that we follow in this volume.

Not all immigration produces diasporas, only those involving the formation of separate communities that result in boundaries between themselves and their host societies and between themselves and other diasporas. These boundaries may be established by the immigrants desiring to maintain their separate identity and distinctive culture in their host country, or they may be imposed by the host society. The large Irish-Catholic migration to the United States during the nineteenth century formed diaspora communities because of the migrants' commitment to a Roman Catholic culture that was alien and believed to be hostile to the prevailing culture of the dominant Protestant establishment. It imposed, in turn, a discriminatory boundary on Irish-Catholic immigrants. Meantime, Scottish and Scots-Irish immigrants, Protestant and English-speaking, blended easily into the majority society and found it unnecessary to form diaspora communities. Racially "visible" and culturally distinctive immigration likely results in diaspora communities, voluntary, imposed, or both. Dark-skinned north African Muslims in France formed or were forced into diaspora communities, while Spanish Catholic immigrants found it unnecessary to resort to diaspora status. Because of their obvious racial and cultural differences, Chinese immigrants in Malaya during the nineteenth century and until World War II formed diaspora communities, while Malay-speaking Muslim immigrants from Indonesia found it unnecessary to do so.

Instead of Cohen's five-part typology – victim, trade, labor, imperial, and cultural – which emphasizes the origin and causes of transnational migrant movements, I find it more useful to limit my taxonomy to three classes – *settler, labor,* and *entrepreneurial* – focusing on the functions they perform in their host country. Thus, a victim diaspora such as Armenians assumes business and professional (entrepreneurial) functions in California. Afro-Caribbeans, regarded by Cohen as a cultural diaspora, become a labor diaspora when they migrate to Britain and North America. The reasons for migrating do not determine or explain the functions that migrants subsequently perform in their host country. These three classes can encompass all transnational migrant communities, historical and contemporary. Migrant communities may include individuals from all social and economic classes, from all walks of life, and with diverse talents and skills. Nevertheless, for analytical purposes, they may be classified according to their *central tendency* based on the predominant function performed by first- and second-generation members in their host country.

While most diasporas remain and expect to remain minority communities in their host country, *settler diasporas* are migrants who arrive with the intention of achieving dominion in their host country. Historical examples are Spanish, French, and English settlers in the Americas, French in Algeria, and Afrikaners in South Africa; more recent examples are Chinese settlers in Tibet and Zionist settlers in Palestine. Since all areas of the earth that are fit for human habitation have already been occupied, however sparsely, by a people and claimed by them as their homeland, settlers must function as conquerors who wrest from another people domination over the territory they have invaded. They may intend originally to achieve domination by peaceful negotiation and assistance to the local people. To justify their invasion and settlement, they may believe that in so doing they are bringing medical, agricultural, or spiritual benefits to the original inhabitants that they subordinate or displace; and that the latter will appreciate and welcome their presence. They may claim prior ownership of the area, more efficient use and exploitation of local resources, or a divinely inspired warrant for their conquering mission.[5] The *conquistadores* in Mexico and Peru looted the wealth of their defeated nations, but claimed that they were bringing them the priceless blessing of eternal salvation by converting them to the true faith.

Labor diasporas are composed mainly of undereducated, unskilled individuals of peasant or urban proletarian backgrounds. They have migrated from their homeland in search of improved livelihoods and better opportunities for their children. As we indicated in chapter 1, they tend not to be the poorest of the poor, since migration requires money to cover transportation and related expenses prior to settlement in their host country. With limited vocational or organizational skills, they gravitate to the lower rungs of the labor force in their host countries, performing hard, dirty, monotonous, and often dangerous tasks for minimal wages. They initially accept lower wages than local workers, for which they are accused of undermining labor standards. The original migrants and their children tend to remain proletarians in their host country, in some cases for several generations until acculturation and education enable them eventually to advance to the middle class and to positions of prestige and power. If they happen to be visible immigrants of different racial stock from the local mainstream, they are vulnerable to discrimination when they attempt to compete for higher-status jobs or better housing. North Africans in France, Turks in Germany, Mexicans in the US, and Afro-Brazilians are contemporary examples of labor diasporas. Irish Catholic migrant communities in North America and Australia are examples of labor diasporas in the nineteenth century.

Entrepreneurial diasporas, by contrast, include a number of individuals with business experience and vocational skills and with some education. Some may be highly educated professionals. The human capital that they have accumulated by education, training and experience provides them with confidence and incentives to seize opportunities that were unavailable to them in their home country, to open businesses, gain skilled employment, or achieve professional positions. Their organizational skills enable them to develop associations that serve the common social, economic, and educational needs of their communities. While they may perforce start their lives in the diaspora in unskilled, low-status, low-wage positions, they are on the lookout for educational or business opportunities. The first and certainly the second generation gain access to education and attain middle-class status in business, skilled labor, and professional roles. They provide role models for their youth. A few become wealthy and influential. If they encounter exclusion or discrimination, they innovate professional roles or discover and exploit niches or high-risk opportunities in the local economy that enable them to practice or further develop their entrepreneurial talents. Overseas Chinese in southeast Asia, Russians in Israel, and Palestinians in Kuwait are examples of entrepreneurial diasporas. The leadership of diaspora communities is drawn from successful business and professional members.

"Middleman minorities" are a sub-class of entrepreneurial diasporas. They comprise business-oriented foreign communities that occupy vacant economic niches between royal, aristocratic, warrior and priestly rulers and the mass of uneducated and unmobilized peasant societies.[6] They construct and operate the wholesale and retail distribution networks for commodities, assume the functions of money lending and banking to the ruling classes and the peasantry, and become skilled craftsmen and manufacturers. Jews, Greeks, and Armenians in the Ottoman Empire, Chinese in southeast Asia, and Indians in east Africa are examples of middleman diasporas. Typically, they remain conspicuously apart from local societies, making no effort to integrate. They maintain social and economic networks with members of their diasporas in other countries.

As these societies gradually modernize and produce indigenous professionals, businesspeople and nationalist intellectuals, the business practices and the very presence of these ethnic outsiders become nationalist targets. The wealth they have accumulated and their high living standards are attacked as being the result of unscrupulous and exploitative business practices. At some point, as the conservative elites who had patronized the middle men, often in response to ill-concealed bribery, lose the ability or the will to protect them, their position becomes increasingly precarious. They may be excluded from certain lines of business, required to accept local "partners," endure violent mob attacks on their persons or property, or even be expropriated and expelled from the country.

Most, but not all diasporas maintain a sympathetic attachment to their former homeland. They remit funds to family members and frequently to their former communities and to causes they favor. They frequently contribute to political changes and to economic development in their former homeland. They may support or they may oppose its present government, extending moral and financial assistance to the side they favor. The diaspora may split into factions, supporting competing parties in their former homeland. They hope to perpetuate their inherited language and culture, even as they adapt to the language and culture of their host country. Interest in their former homeland and culture diminishes with succeeding generations that adapt to the indigenous culture, even when the diaspora maintains or is forced to maintain its boundaries. Relations between diaspora and homeland are further analyzed in chapter 5, which deals with diaspora roles in international relations.

Diaspora communities are not fixed entities. They move through several stages, depending on the changing preferences of their members and the opportunities or restrictions applied by the host government and its dominant society. Both the diasporas' preferences and the policies of host governments may shift over time. With the succession of generations, diasporas become indigenized and may evolve from one category to another. Some members opt out of the diaspora completely, joining the local society. Others evolve hybrid or dual identities, multiple belonging that permits them to evoke the one or the other as situations require. In response, the diaspora's functions, institutions, and services to its members evolve in response to the latter's needs and demands. In the absence of continuing flows of new immigrants, membership and degree of participation may decline as they join the local society, to the point that the diaspora's institutions can no longer be sustained and the diaspora community withers and disappears. Where the opportunity structure remains restrictive and discriminatory, the diaspora may endure, even when most of its members have acculturated to the local patterns and have lost contact with their former homeland. Some of its more imaginative members then create and publicize idealized images of a former, often imagined, homeland to which they dream, one day, of returning.

Information technologies

Diasporas have not escaped the influence of contemporary information technologies (IT). The internet has enabled members of diasporas, through e-mail, to maintain instantaneous and inexpensive communication with family, friends, and business associates in their homeland. Thanks to IT, they have immediate access to newspapers and journals, and thus can follow social, political, and athletic events in their homelands on a daily basis. The net effect is to facilitate transnational existence, especially of the immigrant generation.

Scholars have invented and begun to explore the concept of "digital diasporas."[7] This term refers to diasporas that are organized and sustained through the internet, fostering cyber-communities among individuals of the same ethnic provenance who happen to be scattered geographically. Its proponents argue that digital diasporas can sustain solidarity among their participants, facilitate dialogue, identify areas of agreement and discord, and make it possible for them to interact with their homeland, its government and society, in a coordinated way. Readers may expect empirical testing of the utility of this dimension of IT in the near future.

To summarize this brief chapter: we follow the contemporary definition of diasporas as transnational migrant communities that maintain material or sentimental attachments to their country of origin (their home country) while adapting to the limitations and opportunities available in their host country. To simplify and organize our treatment of diasporas, we classify them regardless of their reason for emigrating, but according to the principal function they perform in their host country as settler, labor, or entrepreneurial types.

As this brief discussion indicates, I treat diasporas as real social categories, similar to other human collectivities such as religious institutions, corporations, and nations that are subject to change over time. I find it unproductive to dispute with social constructionists and other postmodernists who regard all such institutions as intellectual constructs, thus transient, contingent, and deterritorialized, their members shifting their identities as opportunities beckon.[8]

Members of diaspora communities, first-generation immigrants and their offspring, are not disembodied individuals, motivated mainly by personal advantage. Normally they have allegiances to institutions, into which they are socialized, to family, ethnic community, nation, and religion. These attachments bind them into communities that impart meaning and security to their lives. There is nothing transient about these attachments; they cannot readily be abandoned, though individuals may depart from the central tendency of their group. By experience they can learn the benefits of other allegiances which they attempt to reconcile with their original loyalties. In this process they adopt dual or hybrid identities. With succeeding generations these new identities and the lifestyles they involve may eclipse their heritage, which then endures as cultural residues with little effect on day-to-day behavior. Thus, as indicated in chapter 3, Chinese in Bangkok became Thai and Ukrainians in Winnipeg became Canadian. But Chinese in Malaysia remain a separate community, as do north Africans in France.

In chapter 3 we present our data. We describe, analyze, and evaluate the experiences of ten contemporary diaspora communities in Europe, Asia, the Middle East, North and South America. These cases provide the empirical base for comparative treatment that allows for cautious generalization in subsequent chapters.

3

Contemporary case studies

3a. North Africans in France

The western European economies had recovered by 1950 from wartime devastation and stagnation, thanks in large measure to the Marshall Plan. What followed were the two "glorious decades" of rapid and sustained economic growth that yielded widespread prosperity and the generous European welfare states. These ended abruptly with the oil embargo in 1971. Because of their low birth rates, European countries were unable to provide the labor that was required to maintain their economic expansion, especially for the heavier, dirtier, unskilled, low-wage tasks that were increasingly shunned by European workers. These shortfalls in the supply of labor were met by immigration from labor surplus countries, where jobs were scarce and wage rates much lower than those in the booming European economies.

The demand for immigrant labor affected all the economies of western, northern, and central Europe – the Netherlands, Sweden and Austria, as well as the larger economies of Britain, Germany, and France. Italy and Spain, which in the 1950s and 1960s supplied labor to the economies of western Europe, in the 1990s were attracting immigrant labor from the Balkans and from Africa. In Britain and France this demand was met primarily by immigration from their former colonies, for Britain from the Caribbean islands and the Indian subcontinent, for France from the Maghreb and its north African territories, Algeria, Morocco, and Tunisia, which were soon to gain their independence. Germany, with no ex-colonial possessions, recruited actively from Turkey with its large, underemployed peasantry and urban proletariat. Once established in Germany, they came to be known as *Gastarbeiter*, guest-workers, temporary employees who were expected to return to their homeland when their labor was no longer required.

In every European country, these new arrivals formed diaspora communities. Except for financial remittances, brief return visits to family and friends, and continuing interest in the politics of their homelands, the great majority chose to remain in their host country, raise their families, and enjoy a standard of living that would have been unattainable in their erstwhile homeland. Even after economic growth slackened and legal immigration was halted except for family members, while unemployed they could still live comfortably between jobs on payments from their adopted country's generous welfare provisions. Their European-born children, having acculturated to the language and way of life of their host country, had little if any first-hand knowledge of or interest in their ancestral homeland and no desire to "return." Financial incentives offered by several European governments to repatriate fell on deaf ears. While they were needed for their labor, as "visible minorities" with their exotic language, customs, and lifestyles, they were seldom acceptable as fellow citizens. Europeans continued to regard their nations as homogeneous societies with a common White, Christian culture.

The governments of their homelands made no efforts to urge their return. Their financial remittances to family and friends became valuable supplements to the national external accounts. Homeland governments provided special facilities to encourage and enhance the continuing flow of these funds. Accustomed as they had become to European pay scales and welfare benefits, and to democratic practices of free expression, these expatriates could become discontented troublemakers and sources of oppositional politics in their homelands. Better they should remain as emigrants in their European host countries.

When members of these diaspora communities, notably the second, locally born and educated generation, attempted to compete for skilled and professional positions for which they had earned the required qualifications, they frequently encountered discrimination, even systematic exclusion. Though they had every intention of remaining in Europe, they were not acceptable to their European hosts, except as unskilled workers subsisting quietly in their isolated ethnic enclaves. In response, many of them rejected European society, passively in most cases by declining to accept citizenship even when this was possible. In some instances their resentment boiled over into violent protest, culminating in terrorist acts. A prominent theme in their rejection became their attachment to Islam; the more they sensed discrimination and exclusion, the more they emphasized their Islamic identity. They were told by religious leaders, most of whom were trained in and imported from their homelands, that religion and government, church and state, cannot, under Islamic law and practice, be separated. Islam, as they preached it, is incompatible with the infidel, amoral, secular cultures of contemporary Europe. Most European democracies thus confront an unprecedented predicament: permanent ethnic minorities that are socially and politically unacceptable as fellow citizens; thus rejected, they refuse to integrate and become second-class members of the national society and political community; some become openly hostile.

The example that we will analyze is the north African diaspora in France. Five million strong, it now comprises 8 percent of that country's population.

During the nineteenth century, France extended its imperial control over the north African states of Tunisia, Algeria, and Morocco with their Arab-Islamic majorities. Algeria was annexed in 1830 and in 1848 was incorporated as a *département* into metropolitan France, though its inhabitants were not permitted to migrate to the *métropole*. During the early years of the twentieth century, there was a trickle of seasonal labor migration, especially of Berbers from the Kabilya region of Algeria, working mainly in agriculture. They were regarded as sojourners who returned home to their families after the annual French harvest. Finally, in 1914 new legislation enabled Algerians to move to the mainland. The first substantial migration occurred during World War I when an estimated 130,000 north Africans worked in France, mainly in heavy industry and mining. Because of heavy manpower losses during the recent war and its low birth rate, France during the interwar period was chronically short of labor, inducing many north African workers, Muslim and mainly Arab, to remain in France, living in the substandard outskirts (*banlieue*) of the principal industrial centers, Paris, Marseilles, Lyon, and Lille.

Large-scale immigration began about 1950, as the French economy expanded rapidly and its industrial employers recruited workers from the economically depressed north African colonies. These workers found well-compensated, year-round employment, remained permanently in France, joined labor unions, imbibed Marxist and anti-imperialist ideology, and remitted funds to the independence movements in their homelands, including the National Liberation Front (FLN) in Algeria. Beginning in the early 1970s, as the French economy stagnated, the north African diaspora exceeded three million persons. Then, as the French economy began to shift from heavy industry to light manufacturing and services, many found themselves unemployed. But since immigrant workers were entitled to the benefits of France's generous welfare system, including unemployment compensation and child allowances, these provided greater security and higher living standards than they could expect to earn in their native countries. Therefore, most chose to remain in their diaspora communities in France, though few attempted to qualify for naturalization and French citizenship. After 1974, when labor immigration from the former colonies was strictly limited by law, further arrivals consisted of family reunions and illegals. Due primarily to early marriage and very high birth rates, by the turn of the twenty-first century, the north African diaspora numbered five million, 8 percent of France's population.

France's cultural and political elites have long convinced themselves that French culture and political institutions are among the highest achievements of western civilization. Immigrants from other backgrounds, especially Europeans, were welcome, but with the implicit understanding that they would quickly acculturate to the French language, values, and way of life; in effect, become French men and women, committed to the enduring revolutionary principles of liberty, equality, and fraternity, plus *laïcité* (the complete separation of church and state). Poles, Italians, Jews, and Spanish immigrants readily complied with these assimila-tionist strictures. A man with a name like Finkelkraut could be accepted as a leading French philosopher and public intellectual, while a Hungarian immigrant's son named Sarkozy could be elected President of the Republic. French elites also boasted that they, unlike the "Anglo-Saxons," were immune to racist sentiments.

Yet, beneath the surface, ordinary French people harbored deep strains of racist contempt for dark-skinned non-Europeans, demonstrated by their patronizing and frequently abusive treatment of their colonial Algerian and Indo-Chinese subjects. They were especially contemptuous of "dirty, uncivilized Arabs" and hostile to Muslims. Suddenly, after their painful and humiliating losses of Indo-China in 1954 and Algeria in 1962, they were confronted, in the *métropole* itself, with a large, permanently established diaspora of "visible" Muslim ex-colonials. Needed, perhaps, for their labor and tolerated as long as they remained quietly in their *cités* in the suburbs of the major cities, they were otherwise regarded as incapable of assimilation to the French national community, and thus profoundly unwelcome. Repeated incidents of violence during the 1990s confirmed the prevailing hostility toward north African Muslims, provoking threats of tough treatment by French right-wing politicians and numerous deportations of illegal immigrants. A minority of mostly well-educated members of center-left political persuasion attempted to counter the prevailing hostility and discrimination through such defense organizations as SOS-Racisme and measures to prevent police brutality, improve conditions in the *cités*, and encourage members of the second generation of north Africans to exercise their rights as French citizens. They looked forward hopefully to co-opting leaders of these diaspora communities into France's cultural and political institutions; and to the emergence in France of a version of Islam that would be compatible with western principles of human rights and democracy.

Born in France, and therefore French citizens, the second (and third) generations of the north African diaspora were educated in the French national school system, traditionally a major instrument of immigrant acculturation, assimilation, and upward social mobility. Unlike their immigrant parents who, as was common among labor diasporas, were mostly illiterate, they became fluent, fully literate French-speakers. They remained, for the most part, non-observant Muslims, with the same aspirations as other French citizens for good jobs and a comfortable, secular lifestyle. But the lagging development of the French economy after the oil shock of 1973 failed to provide jobs for the mostly unskilled members of the second generation. Their very high rates of chronic unemployment, approaching 50 percent, produced sentiments of resentment, isolation, and powerlessness, and a street culture with the familiar accompaniment of drugs, violence-prone street gangs, petty crime, and hatred of mainstream French society and its representatives – to the point that they harassed and attacked firemen attempting to extinguish fires in their buildings. Despite this harsh environment of overcrowded, rundown public housing and street violence, a minority still managed to complete their secondary education, and earn vocational and professional qualifications.

Yet, many of these fully trained and qualified second-generation north Africans were unable to find employment consistent with their educational credentials. They were forced to accept unskilled jobs, like their immigrant parents, or unemployment. They blamed their blocked careers on the discrimination and institutional racism that kept them segregated and isolated in rundown ghettos. A handful, however, succeeded in local politics, some managed to establish successful businesses catering to the needs of diaspora families, still others built and operated the institutions of a north African musical and artistic subculture that served the second and third generations and became a form of chic for educated French youth. The successful minority who found good jobs tended to move out of the ghettos, take French spouses, and integrate into the mainstream economy, cultural institutions, and political system. But as many as half the inmates in French prisons are of north African origin, and the prisons became recruitment and indoctrination centers for *jihadists*.

During the Algerian conflict from 1954 to 1962, a number of immigrant workers demonstrated in favor of the FLN and for Algerian independence. These demonstrations were ruthlessly suppressed by the police, who regarded such sentiments as treasonous. As they responded to criminal incidents, the police, few of whom were north Africans, were accused of racial profiling, and harsh, abusive, and discriminatory harassment of north African youth. Combined with their demoralizing inability to find employment, police harassment convinced many of these young people that they had been rejected by French society and officialdom, and relegated to marginalized, second-class status, French citizens, but unequal. Their original aspiration to be accepted and included in the national community had been thwarted, leading to bitter resentment, protest, and contempt for all authority. The opportunity structure of the French state and society was judged to be unwelcoming to Muslims of north African origin.

Early in the 1980s, a "National Front" (FN) emerged as a significant force in French political life. Its nativist, xenophobic, and integralist nationalism identifies immigrants, especially "Arabs" as the principal cause of most of their nation's ills, from crime and disease (AIDS) to unemployment and high taxes, mining the state's generous welfare system, including child allowances, which are supplied by taxes extracted from authentic, hard-pressed French working men and women. These "foreigners" in their midst provide an easy scapegoat for their fears and frustrations. The FN advocates summary deportation of illegal immigrants, including non-citizen north Africans, and termination of automatic citizenship for children born of immigrant parents. As the north African "Arab" diaspora can never be assimilated into French society, these foreigners, they argue, should be denied welfare benefits and encouraged to return to their countries of origin. France should be restored to authentic Frenchmen.

With the rise of the National Front, immigration, especially of north Africans, became an important and troublesome issue in French politics. Its candidates, led by the burly ex-paratrooper, Jean-Marie Le Pen, drew between 10 and 20 percent of the vote in local and national elections. Its support base is concentrated among ex-servicemen who fought the losing battles in Vietnam and Algeria, and among former colonists, *pieds noirs*, a million of whom were forced to abandon Algeria after the French withdrawal. It appeals also to small businessmen, former Vichy supporters, and others whose familiar way of life is threatened by globalization and the rationalization of the French economy. Aside from anti-Semitism, the National Front's main tactic is exploiting the fear and anxiety among ordinary French people that this foreign, violent minority that refuses to integrate into French society is undermining their security and the very essence of their nation.

The political left has attempted to resist the growing nativist, anti-immigrant pressures. In 1981, the newly elected Socialist government enacted a law that legalized immigrant associations, stimulating the formation of numerous cultural, recreational, religious, and political organizations within the diaspora. But soon thereafter, in 1986, a center-right government, in order to protect its electoral flank from attack by the National Front, cancelled the automatic grant of citizenship to children of immigrants born in France. Instead, after living in France for five consecutive years between the ages of 13 and 18, they would be required to apply for citizenship.

Initially, the majority of second-generation north Africans, born and educated in France, aspired to participate in the French economy and polity and to be integrated into a French society that would welcome them as equals (according to the principles of *egalité* and *fraternité*, as they were taught), while respecting their distinctive identity and religious practices – even though most were non-observant. The more observant asked and were granted special facilities for prayer in several of the factories, including automobile manufacturing, where they worked. Gradually, however, unemployment, discrimination, and police harassment persuaded many that France had rejected them. This sentiment was dramatically reinforced after October 1989 when the national education authorities refused to allow female Muslim students to wear headscarves in school, as this was held to violate the principle of *laïcité* that banned religious symbols in public institutions. In March 1994, a new law was enacted forbidding the wearing of religious symbols in public schools. This law was interpreted as disrespect for their religion, still another affront by French society to their Arab and Muslim identity. In response, the number of mosques in north African communities multiplied, as did membership in Islamic associations.

Demoralized by unemployment and the grim prospects for their future, angered by the hostile and violent police presence, isolated in their rundown, dehumanizing suburban housing, alienated second-generation north African youth became available for mobilization by newly arrived Muslim clerics, many of them Wahabi trained, who preached that Islam was the answer to all their problems. As Christian France had rejected them, so should they, in the name of Islam, turn their backs on the degenerate, immoral French society and state. Integration into the infidel French society, moreover, would require them to betray their own identity and traditions. Throughout the 1990s, this message resonated with the prevailing depressed and angry mood of second- and third-generation north African youth. In large numbers they declined to claim the French citizenship to which they were entitled. Instead, they embraced Islam as their principal identity and their path to salvation. The Islamist victory in the Algerian election in 1992 and its revocation by the Algerian military, with the obvious support of the French government, provoked demonstrations by north African sympathizers in France and stimulated recruitment into the growing *jihadist* ranks. In 1994, the government established at Nièvre, an Institute of Theology, charged with training a new generation of French-speaking imams to supplant the foreign clerics in the more than 1,200 mosques in France, and to evolve a set of Islamic practices and beliefs compatible with French principles of democracy, human rights, and *laïcité*.

Because of excellent, inexpensive communication and transportation links with nearby north Africa, members of the north African diaspora keep in close touch with family and friends, follow political events in their former homelands, and travel freely back and forth. Some are suspected by French security officials and their north African counterparts of sympathetic links with the Algeria-based Islamist terrorist organization, the Salafist Group for Preaching and Combat (GSPC in French), which is loosely affiliated with Al Qaeda. It has launched numerous suicide and roadside bombs against police stations, power plants, and tourist facilities in Algeria, Morocco, and Tunisia. While GSPC operates mainly in the Maghreb, it is believed to sustain cells among disaffected Muslim youth in Europe, especially in France. Anti-Semitism in contemporary France is largely a north African Muslim phenomenon. They have attacked and burned several Jewish synagogues. Early in March, 2007, a Moroccan court sentenced eight Islamists to 15 years' imprisonment for plotting a series of attacks, including bombing the Paris *métro* and the Orly airport.

Beginning in the 1980s, conditions in the *cités* produced a succession of riots that included the pillaging of shops and especially of public buildings, and violent attacks on Jewish synagogues. These riots were broken up, often with disproportionate violence, by the police. Finally, in October 2005, inflamed by the accidental killing of two north African youngsters, major riots erupted in the *banlieue* outside Paris, spreading rapidly to other centers of north African settlement throughout the country. The violence was highly publicized by the domestic and international media. It resulted in large-scale property damage and injuries, continuing for 20 days until finally brought under control by police measures and exhaustion of the rioters. As many as 10,000 vehicles were torched, 233 public buildings were burned, and 3,200 suspected rioters were arrested. On November 8, after a national state of emergency had been declared by President Chirac, the Minister of the Interior, Nicolas Sarkozy, coining the slogan "love France, or leave it," promised vigorous measures to tighten enforcement of the immigration laws, deport illegals, and revoke the citizenship of agitators who had provoked and prolonged the recent disturbances.

The trauma of October 2005 sent profound shock waves throughout France and, indeed, throughout Europe. Government leaders, influential pundits, and academics were forced to admit that France's immigration policies, including the expectation that north African immigrants would willingly assimilate as equal citizens into the French nation, were in shambles. Compelled, reluctantly, to concede that the large and growing north African Muslim diaspora is in France to stay, neither public opinion nor elites have conceived a program to relieve the prevailing unemployment; nor are they yet prepared to accept the legitimacy of a permanent minority with separate cultural rights (multiculturalism) within the bosom of their Republic. They are unwilling to concede affirmative action – preferential treatment of individuals that would help them integrate into the French economy and society. Nevertheless, some of the elite educational institutions have begun informally to admit a handful of young members of the north African diaspora who would not otherwise qualify for admission. In short, a national consensus on a fresh approach to their north African predicament has not emerged.

The one major city that was spared the demonstrations and riots of October 2005 was Marseilles, where the north African diaspora had been integrated into the political system. Though unemployment remained high, north Africans had been granted ready access to local officials and a forum to voice their grievances and demands. They had not experienced the sense of isolation and powerlessness that was the lot of their compatriots in other French cities.

In October 2006, a year after the riots of October 2005, hooded gangs of young north Africans celebrated the anniversary by attacking and burning buses, cars, and public buildings in several of the nation's suburban slums. During the intervening year, though little had been done by government or private industry to relieve the unemployment, government did launch a major effort to improve the dilapidated high-rise housing estates in the suburban *cités*. The government meanwhile designated no fewer than 751 Sensitive Urban Areas (*Zones Urbaines Sensible*) in the suburbs of the major cities which are believed to be dangerous, no-go areas for the public or even the police. With the breakdown of parental discipline and the absence of a police presence, these areas are controlled by north African criminal gangs. On March 27, 2007, a gang of 300 north African youth fought a seven-hour battle with police at Paris's Gare du Nord railway station before order could be restored. Police training and equipment have been upgraded, an anti-discrimination agency has been established, and the major political parties for the first time included north Africans as candidates for Parliament in the spring 2007 elections. Meanwhile, north Africans' sense of isolation, exclusion from the economy, and powerlessness remain. They continue to be conspicuously absent from elite circles in French government, politics, industry, universities, and cultural institutions. President Sarkozy made a surprising breakthrough, however, appointing Rachida Dati, daughter of north African immigrants, to the prestigious post of Justice Minister.

On February 8, 2008, more than two years after the October 2005 riots, President Sarkozy issued a five-point, three-year "Marshall Plan" for improving the opportunity structure for the youth of France's north African diaspora. Some 4,000 additional police officers would be assigned to suburban posts to insure order, job training would be provided for 100,000 young north Africans, "second chance" schools would be available for former dropouts to enable the brightest among them to qualify for universities and the *grandes écoles*, new transportation links would be built to enable residents of the suburbs to get to their new jobs, and finally, a "merciless war" would be initiated against drug dealers. Skeptics doubt that President Sarkozy can find the money to finance and implement these expensive initiatives.[1] They also question how residents of the *cités* will respond to these gestures from the man who had recently referred to them as "scum."

As with any large community, the north African diaspora is and will remain far from monolithic. Some of its members struggle to earn the credentials that, with luck, will enable them to gain access to the institutions of the French economy or government, accept French citizenship, and graduate out of the ghettos and into the mainstream. Others set up and operate businesses or cultural agencies that serve the large north African public. Still others, especially women, who are more pragmatic and appreciate the rights available to women in French society, find jobs in the lower rungs of the nation's manufacturing and commercial labor force and eventually earn upward mobility. The central tendency, however, is acculturation to the French language and way of life, accompanied by alienating unemployment, rejection of French citizenship, and, for some, espousal of militant versions of Islam that are incompatible with the established tenets of French national life.

They are convinced that their unemployment, blocked career aspirations, and marginalization are the result of discrimination that is condoned by the majority of French officialdom and public. The election in May 2007, as

President of the Republic, of Nicolas Sarkozy, who built his reputation as the formidable enemy of immigrant violence, confirmed their belief that France rejects them. Some observers regard France's alienated north African youth as a ticking time bomb for the French state. As the opportunity structures of the French economy, government, and society have blocked their career aspirations, disrespected their religion and culture, and demonstrated hostility to their diaspora, in response they have turned their backs on France. North African Muslims remain in France, but not of France.

3b. Overseas Chinese: Malaysian, Thai, Japanese

The Chinese diaspora is a major presence and actor in Malaysia and Thailand. In Malaysia it comprises about 25 percent of the population; in Thailand it makes up 11 percent of a much larger society. Yet, the experience and prospects of these communities differ in fundamental respects, illustrating one of the main themes of this study.

Chinese traders were active in southeast Asia from the sixteenth century, establishing posts in its major port cities, notably Malaka in Malaya and Batavia in Java. Some returned home after making their fortunes, but many remained, marrying local women, adapting to local customs, but maintaining their Chinese identity. These included the "Baba" Chinese of Malaka who, four centuries later, assumed a leading role in Malayan Chinese politics at the time of Malayan independence. The Ch'ing (Manchu) dynasty in China (1644–1911) forbad and criminalized emigration until late in the nineteenth century. Nevertheless thousands managed to emigrate as traders, small businessmen, and laborers. Despite occasional pogroms, especially in the Philippines, they established themselves as middleman minorities in and around the major cities in southeast Asia and prospered. During the nineteenth century and until World War II, economic expansion in all the European colonies required laborers, skilled craftsmen, and local merchants. These roles were filled mainly by

Chinese immigrants who were regarded by both European officialdom and native elites as sojourners (guest workers) who remained Chinese nationals; when their work was done, they would return to China, as many did. (China's governments, imperial as well as republican, adhered to the principle of ius sanguinis, regarding all ethnic Chinese, wherever they happened to be located, as permanent Chinese nationals and subjects of the Chinese state.[2] The European colonial powers acquiesced in this policy).[3]

Most of these émigrés, however, chose to remain permanently, establishing separate residential enclaves (Chinatowns), social and cultural associations and institutions, such as schools, temples, burial associations, shops offering Chinese products, and restaurants specializing in Chinese cuisine to meet their individual and collective needs. Criminal organizations, including the notorious triads, practicing extortion and operating protection rackets, flourished in these communities, despite harassment by the colonial police. These diaspora communities constituted one element in the plural societies of southeast Asia, leading separate existences, interacting with the indigenous society mainly through economic transactions in the marketplace.[4] In 1999, there were an estimated 34.5 million overseas Chinese.[5]

During the colonial era, the major mining, plantation, banking and trading enterprises were owned and operated by Europeans, Chinese serving as subaltern clerks, craftsmen, and wholesale and retail distributors. As a classical "middleman minority," Chinese occupied economic niches between colonial enterprises and the mass of native peasants.[6] Some of the more enterprising Chinese succeeded in establishing their own smaller mining, plantation, trading and banking businesses, and some became wealthy. What developed was an ethnic division of labor: colonialists owning and managing the larger economic enterprises, as well as government, military, and police agencies; natives as small-holder peasants, fishermen, and unskilled workers; Chinese as wholesale and retail merchants, money lenders, skilled craftsmen, mechanics, clerks, food processors, and small manufacturers. As the colonialists gradually departed after World War II, Chinese became their residual legatees, owning and operating a very large percentage of the economies of every southeast Asian country. The major southeast Asian transnational enterprises were created and managed by Chinese, usually by extended networks of family members residing in several east and southeast Asian countries. Economically powerful, overseas Chinese were politically vulnerable, easy targets and scapegoats for aspiring native politicians and frustrated intellectuals.

Chinese nationalism emerged after the humiliating defeat of the Imperial armies by the Japanese in 1895, followed by the overthrow of the Imperial regime in 1911 by the nascent republican movement. The republican Kuo Min-tang (KMT) party, espousing Chinese nationalism, sent teachers and political agents to spread the nationalist gospel among their overseas compatriots and to raise funds to support its armed forces. After the 1920s, the Chinese Communist Party dispatched its own agents to compete with the KMT for the support of the increasingly prosperous overseas Chinese communities. Their anti-imperialist message aroused suspicion among the colonial authorities, inviting counter-measures up to and including jailing and deportation. After Japan invaded China in 1931, overseas Chinese participated in the anti-Japanese struggle by sending money to the resistance forces and by boycotting Japanese products in their wholesale and retail businesses.

Chinese in Malaya/Malaysia

In Malaya the British colonial authorities regarded themselves as patrons and protectors of Malays, the indigenous people, their culture and social systems. Chinese were considered resident aliens, economic sojourners who would one day return to China. For example, the schooling of Chinese children was provided not by government, but by Christian missionaries or by the Chinese themselves. Christian missionaries were not permitted to proselytize among Malaya's Muslims.

During World War II most native elites in southeast Asia, including Malays, cooperated with the Japanese military who occupied their countries. The Japanese treated them respect-fully, promising them early independence from the European imperialists within the Japanese-led East Asia Co-prosperity Sphere. By contrast, Chinese were regarded as enemy aliens, forced to pay special taxes and make "voluntary" contribu-tions to the Japanese war effort, while their young men were mobilized into labor gangs to work on Japanese projects in Malaya and elsewhere in southeast Asia. Led by cadres of the Malayan Communist Party (MCP), Chinese youth formed a resistance army, the Malayan People's Anti-Japanese Army (MPAJA), mounting an insurgency that sabotaged Japanese facilities and established contacts with Australian and British forces. When the British returned after the Japanese surren-der and resumed colonial rule, the Communist insurgents refused to disband or surrender their weapons. In 1948, as instructed by Moscow, the MCP resumed its insurgency, this time against the British imperialists. The insurgency, led and manned by Chinese with no Malay participation, raged for more than a decade. It was finally suppressed in 1960 after a lengthy and very costly counter-insurgency campaign by British-led Australian, Malayan, and British forces.

During the "Emergency," a half-million rural and small-town Chinese were rounded up and confined into a series of walled and gated "new villages" to cut off recruitment and logistical assistance to the insurgents. To provide charitable relief and assistance to the displaced and impecunious new villagers, a group of wealthy Chinese organized the Malayan Chinese Association (MCA), which soon became the leading representative for non-Communist Chinese. Meantime, to resist and defeat the British proposal for a Malayan Union, which would have diminished the political role of the Malay aristocracy and eliminated the "special position" (in effect, preferences) for indigenous Malays, a group of Malay aristo-crats and school teachers organized a United Malays National Organization (UMNO). After its success in defeat-ing the Malayan Union scheme in the British parliament, an agreement was negotiated with the MCA and the smaller Malayan Indian Congress (MIC), with the blessing of the British, to form a conservative multi-ethnic political movement, the Alliance Party, that would lead the nation to independence in 1957.

Under the terms of this inter-ethnic bargain, Malays would control government, Islam would be the state religion, Malay the national language, and the head of state would be a Malay Sultan, rotated for five-year terms among the several Malay royal families. Special measures would be authorized to raise the educational level of Malays and increase their participation in the modern sectors of the economy. Non-Malays born in Malaya would gain full citizenship, enjoy economic and religious freedom, and participate as junior partners in government.[7] This UMNO–MCA–MIC Alliance, now the National Front, has governed Malaya (expanded in 1962 into Malaysia) since 1955, winning every election.[8] It established a pattern of ethnic politics in which the governing parties and the opposition parties speak for and represent only their ethnic constituents. There have been no significant multiethnic or non-ethnic parties. Until 1970 Malaysia functioned as a consociational polity.[9]

Following violent disturbances after elections in May 1969, UMNO reinforced the political dominance of Malays, including the status of the national language. The positions of Prime Minister, Deputy Prime Minister, and senior ministerial positions are held exclusively by Malays. A 4:1 ratio of Malays to non-Malays prevails in the administrative and diplomatic services of the national bureaucracy; Malays firmly control the army and the national police. As the state religion, Islam has in recent years been emphasized by UMNO in order to compete with the principal Malay opposition party, the Islam Party (PAS), which promises to convert Malaysia into an Islamic state. Malay preferences and quotas are enforced in higher education and government employment. Since 1970, the New Economic Policy (NEP) has used the authority of government to expand Malay ownership of shares and management participation in modern banking, industrial and commercial enterprises, and in the learned professions; similar measures apply to foreign-owned corporations. The MCA remains a junior partner in government, while the main Chinese opposition party, the Democratic Action Party (DAP), representing Chinese professionals and workers, advocates a non-ethnic, meritocratic society. (Its preferred slogan, a "Malaysian Malaysia," has been declared subversive, as it challenges the special position of Malays.) DAP accuses the MCA of caring only for its financiers and capitalist supporters, and failing to stand up for the rights of rank-and-file non-Malays.

Though blocked in some sectors of industry by the NEP, Chinese-owned enterprises have expanded with the fast-growing Malaysian economy. According to recent estimates, Chinese now own and control about 60 percent of the national economy (excluding land, which is owned mainly by Malays). Their per capita income remains double that of their Malay compatriots. Nevertheless, Chinese complain of continuing government discrimination in higher education and of burdensome economic restrictions, including discrimination against Chinese firms competing for government contracts. They have been unsuccessful in urging government to terminate the NEP's economic preferences for Malays. Though economically prosperous, Malaysian Chinese regard themselves as politically powerless, marginalized second-class citizens. They can only watch from the sidelines as Malays debate among themselves whether Malaysia has or should become an Islamic state. During the past half-century, there has been a steady trickle of Indonesian immigrants into Malaysia. They have been incorporated without ceremony into Malay-Muslim society and qualify as *bumiputera*, native sons. Chinese born in Malaysia, whose forebears arrived long before many of the ex-Indonesians, are excluded from the status and privileges of native sons. Though citizens, they are forever outsiders, excluded from mainstream society.

Chinese-language elementary schools continue to educate Chinese children through the sixth grade, after which students transfer to secondary and university schooling, mainly in the national language, Malay. Some instruction, especially in the sciences, continues to be in English. There are also expensive private schools and Chinese have recently been authorized to establish a private university, since the current quota system denies many qualified Chinese students entry into the national universities. Socially, the two ethnic communities maintain separate existences. Chinese continue to regard their culture as far superior to the Malay. There is virtually no intermarriage, since this would require the Chinese partner to convert to Islam. Even when Chinese do convert, as few have, they do not become Malay, do not qualify as *bumiputera*, and thus are not entitled to the many educational and economic privileges available to Malays, but denied to non-Malays. Chinese are frequently reminded that Malays are the indigenous people, while they are merely immigrants. Though on the surface interethnic relations remain mostly civil and respectful, there are palpable underlying tensions and distrust between Malays and Chinese.[10] Malaysia remains a plural society. The boundary between Malay society and the Chinese diaspora is rigidly maintained. This is reflected in the organization of politics into rigidly separate ethnic parties.[11]

A number of Malaysian Chinese protest against discriminatory treatment, especially in higher education, by emigrating, mainly to industrialized English-speaking countries, including Singapore, Australia, Canada, and the United States. The steady trickle of emigrants from Malaysia during the past three decades now totals 1.5 million, mostly Chinese.[12] The MCA has attempted to organize MCA clubs in centers of Malaysian emigration to maintain their connections with the homeland and prevent further erosion of Malaysia's Chinese community, its constituency. It urges emigrants to reverse the brain drain and return to their prosperous homeland. Having benefited from non-discriminatory educational, professional, and business opportunities, and having established families in their adopted countries, few show any inclination to return. They do, however, maintain communication and financial links with relatives and friends.

The Sino-Thai diaspora

During the nineteenth century, Thailand experienced economic colonization, mainly by British plantation, mining, trading, and banking interests, but escaped political colonization. The need to prevent colonial intrusion occasioned the faint beginnings, about 1850, of modern Thai nationalism. At the same time, King Chulalongkorn, who reigned from 1870 to 1910, readily acknowledged the Chinese element in his family's origins. He welcomed Chinese immigrants for their contribution to the economic development of his kingdom, employing a group of privileged Chinese as tax farmers. The second decade of the twentieth century witnessed the expansion of modern Chinese nationalism, as the republican forces under Dr Sun Yat-sen, with generous financing from the overseas Chinese diaspora, overthrew the decadent Ch'ing dynasty. Soon Thailand's Chinese became embroiled in the bitter competition between the nationalist KMT and the Communists. During the 1930s they united in opposing Japan's incursions into China by remitting funds to aid the anti-Japanese resistance and by boycotting Japanese goods.

In 1911, the new king, Vajiravudh, infused by his European education with western concepts of ethnic nationalism and outraged by a strike of Chinese merchants protesting a small increase in their tax rate, initiated a new phase of Thai nationalism. This was intended to counteract what the King believed to be the rising threat of Chinese chauvinism among foreigners in his kingdom, who happened to control large slices of the national economy. His two pamphlets, *The Jews of the Orient* (1914) and *Cogs in Our Wheels* (1915) aimed to alert the native population to the Chinese threat.[13] They emphasized that the essence of Thai nationality was and must remain loyalty to the nation, the Theravada Buddhist faith, and the king (*chart, sasana, phra mahakasat*). Chinese were resident foreigners. A number of measures were enacted to limit and restrain their economic activity, but these were indifferently enforced and easily evaded.

The dictatorship of Phibul-songkram, beginning in 1938, fostered serious measures to undermine the Chinese grip on the national economy and encourage assimilation. A number of occupations were closed to Chinese; Chinese associations, including the secret societies, were placed under control of the military. Many were closed altogether, and their activists deported. Chinese-language newspapers were suppressed and Chinese-language schools were closed. They were allowed to reopen only when they had converted the medium of instruction to Thai; Chinese-language training was strictly limited. When, during World War II, Phibul aligned Thailand with Japan, his country escaped the harsh Japanese occupation that was visited on its neighbors, the former European colonies. Chinese businessmen, however, were compelled to cooperate with the Japanese by providing supplies at bargain prices, while secretly finding ways to remit funds to the Chinese national army.

Immigration from China was curtailed, and after the Communist victory in 1949 entirely eliminated. The government and the military founded and operated a number of industries in order to counteract Chinese domination of the economy. The government assumed a militant anti-Communist posture, refusing to recognize the Maoist regime in China, and joining the US-sponsored Southeast Asia Treaty Organization (SEATO), headquartered in Bangkok. The Thai Communist Party, manned almost entirely by Chinese, was outlawed and its low-intensity insurrection confined to northern Thailand. It was sustained by the Beijing government until 1979 when aid was terminated. Thereafter, the waning Communist cadres attempted to support themselves by drug trafficking. Chinese were encouraged to learn and speak Thai; operate their businesses in the Thai language; adopt Thai surnames; and adhere to the Buddhist faith. Continued expressions of Chinese nationalism would be regarded as subversive and were, of course, bad for business. After a series of indecisive measures, the Nationality Act of 1956 finally awarded citizenship to persons of Chinese origin who were born and continued to reside in the kingdom.

The government's persistent and patient policy of induced acculturation and assimilation has paid off. Thai-born Chinese now identify politically as Thai, speak and work in the Thai medium, have taken Thai surnames, and have adopted the Thai version of Buddhism. Many have inter-married with Thai partners. After 1980, the government relaxed its anti-Chinese measures, allowing increased Chinese language instruction in secondary schools and uni-versities. Much of the Thai economy remains in the hands of Sino-Thai, who also participate actively in public affairs. The recent Prime Minister, Thaksin Shinawatra, a tycoon in the communications industry, is a Sino-Thai as were two of his recent predecessors. The present generation of Sino-Thai identify as loyal Thai and are so regarded by their Thai compatriots. While some have fully assimilated culturally and socially, in their homes and in their communities the majority continue to celebrate traditional Chinese festi-vals and observe traditional religious rites. Recognizing that remaining as resident foreigners would subject them to numerous disabilities, and that the pathway was clear for them to integrate into the Thai polity and society, they have taken full advantage of Thailand's open opportunity structure.[14]

While members of the large Chinese diaspora in Thailand, now in the third and fourth generations, retain vestiges of their ancestral culture in their homes, they have integrated into Thai society and adopted a firm Thai political identity. They play prominent roles in higher education, the profes-sions, cultural institutions, national politics, and, of course, the national and regional economy. Several of the Sino-Thai business syndicates participate actively as investors and traders in mainland China's burgeoning post-Maoist economy. In recent years, with a growing sense of security as Thai citizens, some have begun openly to celebrate cultural events, such as Chinese New Year.[15]

Contrast their successful integration into and acceptance

by Thai society and polity with the continuing predicament of Malaysia's Chinese. Once they agreed to speak and work in Thai, adopt Thai surnames, and observe the Buddhist faith – in effect, to assimilate into Thai society – the opportunity structure was open to them. The boundary between Thai and Sino-Thai is diminishing. In neighboring Malaysia, the opportunity structure enables the Chinese diaspora to enjoy economic prosperity, but compels them to remain a separate, socially and politically marginalized community.

Chinese labor diaspora in Japan

Affluent and insular Japan is the world's second largest economy. Its population peaked at 128 million in 2004, but if current demographic trends, including an aging population and a very low birth rate, continue, it is projected to drop below 90 million within 50 years and fall to 40 million by the end of the century. Japan is already experiencing chronic labor shortages, especially in low-wage, unskilled occupations in manufacturing, restaurants, hotels, hospitals, domestic service, landscaping, construction, entertainment, and the sex industries. Employers in manufacturing industries clamor for additional labor; some have "outsourced" their operations to low-wage countries. Japan's pension systems urgently require substantial additional influxes of funds, which could be provided, in part, by contributions from young foreign workers.

The national government welcomes non-citizen professionals and technicians, but continues to insist that Japan is not a country of immigration and must remain a homogenous society of the Yamato race. It does not welcome immigrant laborers. The great majority of Japanese, with little experience in dealing with outsiders (*gaijin*), tend to be intolerant of and uncomfortable with foreigners.

At present, there are a conservatively estimated two million non-citizens in Japan. About 400,000 are ethnic Koreans, whose grandparents were brought to Japan as laborers during the Pacific War. Now in their third and fourth generation, they are denied Japanese citizenship. Excluded from many employment opportunities, they are prominent in a number of marginal activities, including operation of the popular *pachinko* (pinball) parlors, and are suspected by many as harboring criminal tendencies, including participation in the *Yakuza* criminal syndicates. Other non-citizens are recruited by contractors, who hire them out to employers. For such workers, deemed "casual," employers are not required to provide health, disability, pension, or other welfare benefits. Many suffer abuses, including unsafe working conditions, substandard wages, lengthy hours of work, child labor, and, for female workers, sexual harassment. Any complaints or protests carry the risk of deportation. They are widely suspected by the Japanese public of criminal tendencies and of having "sneaked" into the country.

Some of these workers enter Japan legally as students, trainees, or interns, enrolling in language or vocational schools which are only lightly regulated. Attracted to Japan by high wages, they join the casual labor force. They then overstay their visas. Others enter illegally. Responding to pressure from employers, local governments arrange for the housing, healthcare, and schooling of immigrant workers and their children, while the police turn a blind eye to the presence of these incipient diasporas, unless they engage in criminal activities. Tokyo has provided small grants to local authorities to assist in financing these services. Japan's labor unions have attempted, so far unsuccessfully, to organize members of this shadow labor force.

If Japan is to maintain its present population, meeting its demand for labor, sustaining domestic markets for its industries, and financing its pension funds, it must accommodate an additional 600,000 immigrants a year.[16] Yet, current estimates indicate annual arrivals at only 70,000. The majority of non-citizen workers currently in Japan are believed to be Chinese, because of China's proximity and the sharp difference in wage rates in the two economies. Chinese immigrants can readily pass for Japanese and are better equipped than other Asians to master the Japanese language. At present they are tolerated only as a source of cheap labor, with no civil rights, no future prospect of integration into Japanese society, and no pathway to eventual citizenship for themselves or their locally born children.[17]

After two decades in which this problem failed to be acknowledged, the question of immigration is now vigorously debated in the national media. The *Keidanren*, spokesmen for Japan's larger employers, has presented several proposals for increasing the annual intake of immigrant workers and providing for their care. Their proposal envisages a system of rotation, treating them as guest workers temporarily in Japan. It would provide needed labor, while preventing their integration into Japanese society.

Notwithstanding these demographic and economic realities, the Tokyo government remains resolutely in denial. It refuses to face up to the dimensions of its requirements for immigrant labor. It makes no provision for the orderly reception and maintenance of urgently needed migrant labor, for the status of diaspora communities, for their eventual integration into Japanese society, or for their achievement of citizenship. Nor does it prepare the Japanese public for the toleration of ethnic diversity or for the proper treatment and welcoming of transnational immigrants, whose contributions are essential to the maintenance of Japan's economy. The labor diasporas in Japan, including Chinese, remain an economically essential, but socially excluded and politically non-existent, underground presence.

In this section we have analyzed the experience of Chinese immigrants in three Asian countries on the periphery of the Middle Kingdom. The majority of these migrants were unskilled peasants from China's southeast coastal provinces. Yet, as the diaspora communities that they formed encountered different opportunity structures, their fate has differed accordingly. In Malaysia and Thailand, those with business skills or inclinations responded to the need for middlemen, and later for domestic capitalists, and became the economic elite that made indispensable contributions to the expansion and modernization of these economies. But socially and politically, they encountered divergent opportunities. In Malaysia, though citizens, they have been required to remain a separate community, economically prosperous, but excluded socially and marginalized politically. By contrast, after several decades of official suspicion, in Thailand they have responded to the opportunity for acculturation and assimilation to Thailand's political and societal mainstream. In Japan, where their experience is too brief to allow for evaluation, they are likely to remain a labor diaspora. As Japan is already well stocked with vigorous entrepreneurs, it seems unlikely that many Chinese immigrants will be able to challenge them. There is no need in Japan for a middle-man minority. Their path to upward mobility in Japan, once their status has been legalized, will be through education and acquired technical and professional skills.

Three diaspora communities, similar in origins and talents, but different outcomes. How can the differences be accounted for? The critical factor seems to lie not in any attributes of the diasporas, but in the radically different opportunities they encountered in these three countries.

3c. Zionists in Palestine

During the many centuries of their exile from Palestine, their promised land, following their defeats by Roman legions in AD 70 and 135, members of the Hebrew diaspora yearned in their prayers for divine deliverance and return, one day, to Jerusalem, their holy city. In their exile, they were scattered over many lands in western and eastern Europe, the Middle East, and north Africa. While many converted, often forcibly, to the faith of their Christian and Muslim neighbors and blended into their societies, the majority, enduring episodes of persecution, clung to their faith and the promise of messianic redemption in Jerusalem. What maintained their cohesion through the many centuries of their exile was a set of laws and practices derived from the Torah, biblical revelation that underlay their religion of ethical monotheism.

Origins of the Zionist state

The nineteenth century was an era of ethnic nationalism in Europe. It held that every distinctive cultural community should enjoy the right to constitute itself a nation and form an independent, self-governing state on the territory inhabited by its people. Small groups of Jewish intellectuals began to argue that of all European peoples, they alone had no land in Europe that they could call their own. Thus, they were condemned to be strangers, suspect and subject to oppression, in countries and on the territory belonging to other nations. Jews, they proclaimed, must cease being a people who survive by the sufferance of others, and become instead a normal nation that manages its own affairs on its own land.

The Dreyfus affair in France in the 1890s sent shockwaves through Jewish circles in Europe.[18] If France, the most liberal European state, author of the Universal Declaration on the Rights of Man, could generate such blatant anti-Semitism, where could Jewish minorities be safe anywhere in their exile? And so, in the writing, diplomacy, and organizational skills of the assimilated Viennese journalist, Teodor Herzl, the modern Zionist movement was born. The Jewish diaspora, its spokesmen announced, is an ancient people entitled to the right of self-determination, but deprived of its own land. They must reinvent themselves as a normal nation, possessing their own land, with their own language that must be biblical Hebrew, not Yiddish, the language of their European exile. Though sparsely populated sites in east Africa and Latin America were briefly considered, they concluded that their land must be Palestine, centered on Jerusalem, their promised land, the site of their ancient capital and holy places.[19]

The slow and patient process of colonizing Palestine, then held by the decaying Ottoman Empire, was undertaken by Zionist pioneers, mostly from eastern Europe. Funds were raised to purchase and reclaim land, parcel by parcel, from Turkish and Arab landowners. Groups of pioneers were organized to form settlements under arduous conditions. Jewish labor and modern farming practices, they asserted, would make the deserts bloom. "A land without people for a people without land" was a common slogan. But an awkward fact soon confronted them: there was another people on the land they coveted. To this unpleasant reality, Zionists replied that local Arabs would welcome Jewish colonization, since the modern medical and agricultural methods introduced by the Zionist settlers would greatly improve the living standards and quality of life of their Arab neighbors.

During the first quarter of the twentieth century, Zionists constituted a tiny, but active minority of the Jewish diaspora in Europe and North America. A faction of the religiously orthodox, mainly in eastern Europe, regarded Zionism as a heresy, since Jews should expect to return to Zion only when the Lord had revealed his chosen one to inaugurate the messianic age for Jews and for all mankind. Until then, they must wait patiently for their redemption. Most emancipated Jews in western Europe and North America regarded themselves as a religious community, not a nation in exile; they aspired to be regarded as loyal citizens of the nation state in which they resided. Fearful of the charge of dual loyalty, they rejected Zionism. The substantial Jewish communities in the Middle East and North Africa were largely untouched by modern Zionism, which remained a European movement. The Zionist movement reflected many of the cleavages within European Jewry. Among the major parties, all of which were ardent Jewish nationalists, the dominant faction were Labor Zionists intent on creating a secular socialist workers' paradise, culturally European, in their new homeland. General Zionists represented business-oriented groups. Religious Zionists hoped to found a nation in which religious laws and practices would be officially enforced. Revisionists, so called, advocated aggressive nationalism – direct action through military means to found a Jewish state that would encompass all of mandate Palestine.

The Balfour Declaration and its aftermath

The first favorable break in their struggle for recognition occurred during World War I, when the embattled British government in November 1917, hoping to enhance its support for America's entry into the war among Zionist sympathizers in the United States, issued the Balfour Declaration. It stated simply that the British government would "view with favour the establishment in Palestine of a national home for the Jewish people," but without prejudice to the "civil and religious rights of existing non-Jewish communities."[20]

At the conclusion of the war and dissolution of the defeated Ottoman Empire, the fledgling League of Nations awarded Britain a mandate over Palestine. The mandate incorporated the terms of the Balfour Declaration, providing international legitimacy to the Zionist enterprise. During the succeeding two decades, protected by British rule, this settler diaspora was able, very slowly and gradually, to expand its settlements and build the shadow institutions, political, economic, social, and military, of the future Zionist state. These included its militia, the Haganah. Persecution by the Nazi regime in Germany brought to Palestine significant additions of highly skilled professionals and businessmen. They established cultural and scientific institutions, including the Israel Philharmonic, the Hebrew University of Jerusalem, the Weitzman Institute for Scientific Research, and the Technion, a sophisticated engineering school. They built the rudiments of an industrial base that later expanded into world-class high-tech pharmaceutical, computer software, medical instrumentation, and weapons manufacturing. Nevertheless, at the outbreak of hostilities in Europe in 1939, after a half-century of effort, the Zionist community in Palestine, numbering little more than a half-million, constituted a mere 3 percent of world Jewry.

During this period, as Arab resistance was mobilized in response to the growing Zionist presence, Palestinian nationalism was born. Organized violence broke out in 1920,

1929, and especially in the Arab Revolt from 1936 to 1939, targeting Zionist settlements. The Arab Revolt was finally repressed by British forces, but its intensity, plus the demands of Middle East Arab governments, persuaded London that it could no longer honor the Balfour Declaration. Further Jewish immigration would have to be curtailed. The consequence was that during World War II, which witnessed widespread persecution of European Jews, culminating in the European Holocaust in the vast territories overrun by Hitler's armies, this refuge for oppressed Jews was closed. Zionists, nevertheless, cooperated with the British military in its Middle East operations, gaining valuable military experience, while the Arab leadership accepted the patronage of Nazi Germany. Painfully aware of the abandonment and ongoing persecution of stranded Jews in postwar Europe, the Zionist movement concluded that nothing short of statehood would make it possible for its community in Palestine to open its doors to the remnants of the Nazi Holocaust.

Weary of mediating the conflict between Zionists and Palestinians and bankrupted by its wartime struggle, Britain informed the newly established United Nations Organization that it would abandon its mandate and leave Palestine in May 1948. A UN Commission, convinced that Jews and Arabs could not coexist peacefully in the same territory, designed a scheme, similar to a plan drawn up a decade earlier by the British Peel Commission. Palestine would be partitioned into a Jewish and a Palestinian region; Jerusalem would be administered as an international trusteeship. Zionists, now 600,000 strong, eagerly accepted the plan, as it would grant their aspiration for statehood, even though it fell far short of their territorial demands; Arabs rejected it, as they had rejected the Peel recommendation. Zionism, their spokesmen argued, was no more or less than latter-day European colonialism, violating Arab and Muslim lands for European settlement. Since Arabs were in no way responsible for the European Holocaust, why should they be required to pay the price for its consequence?

The Founding of Israel and of the PLO

As the British withdrew, hostilities broke out between Zionists and Palestinians, the latter supported by the armies of the six surrounding Arab states. A number of war veterans from the American Jewish diaspora joined the Israeli fighting forces, of whom the best known was US Regular Army Colonel David (Micky) Marcus. After helping the Haganah develop its strategy, Marcus lost his life in combat. After a year of bloody struggle, in which Israeli casualties totaled 1 percent of its population, the UN succeeded in brokering an armistice. The military borders established by this armistice became the de facto boundaries of Israel, the independent Zionist state. The area east of Israel, including part of Jerusalem and its holy sites, was annexed to Jordan; the Gaza strip was held by Egypt. After strenuous efforts by the Jewish diaspora in the United States, independent Israel was recognized by President Truman. This was followed in short order by the Soviet Union and most European states. Israel was then admitted to the United Nations. None of the Arab governments or non-aligned states recognized Israel.[21]

According to UN estimates, 726,000 Palestinians abandoned their homes in Israel or were driven out by the Israeli military and became refugees in neighboring Arab countries, subsisting in encampments administered by the UN Relief and Works Agency (UNRWA). Except for Jordan, which conferred citizenship on Palestinians within its jurisdiction, Arab countries that hosted Palestinian refugees confined them to refugee enclaves, denied them local employment, and nursed their desire for revenge, insisting on their right of return to reclaim their former homes in Palestine. By the turn of the twenty-first century, their numbers had increased to 4.6 million, of whom more than a million remain in UNRWA-administered camps. Zionist sources report that an estimated 900,000 Jews, deprived of their property and forced to flee Muslim countries where they had resided for centuries, sought refuge in Israel, an even greater number than the Palestinians who left Israel. The result, they held, was a coerced population exchange, canceling any legitimate Palestinian claims of a right of return.

Two decades later, Palestinians in exile, led by Yasir Arafat, formed the Palestine Liberation Organization (PLO), dedicated to recovering their lost homeland by any possible means, including the hijacking of airlines and other attacks against Israeli and Jewish targets. The PLO was a federation of several Palestinian organizations, ranging from Marxist to Islamist.[22] They competed for support among the Palestinian and wider Arab publics and Arab and Muslim governments. The largest organization was Fatah, headed by Arafat, espousing secular nationalism. Outside the PLO was the Islamist Hamas, advocating the creation within liberated Palestine of an Islamic state. Hamas, which received financial and military support from Syria and Iran, was branded a terrorist organization by the United States and European Union. When Arafat accepted the Oslo compromise in 1994, by which Israel and the PLO committed themselves to mutual recognition, Hamas continued to urge the destruction of Israel by armed force. After the death of Arafat, and Israel's withdrawal from the Gaza strip, Fatah and Hamas became embroiled in an armed struggle for control of the embryonic Palestinian state. Palestine had became the object of psychological, diplomatic, and armed conflict between two national movements, Jewish and Palestinian, both claiming sovereignty over the same territory.

Majority and minority

Immediately following independence, Israel's parliament conferred Israeli citizenship on any Jew who chose to exercise the "right of return" to the Jewish homeland. During the next few years, Israel's settler diaspora received and absorbed two streams of immigrants that quadrupled its Jewish population: Holocaust survivors from the displaced persons camps in Europe, and "Sephardim" from long-standing Jewish communities in the Middle East and north Africa, where they were no longer welcome. During the

1990s, after the collapse of the Soviet Union, an additional million "Russians," some with questionable Jewish credentials, made their way to Israel. At the turn of the twenty-first century, the Jewish population of Israel leveled off at about 5.5 million. It was no longer a pioneering society of agricultural settlers. Supplemented by well-educated immigrants, its universities produced scientists, engineers, professionals, and businesspeople who achieved the high level of economic development that enabled most Israelis to enjoy a comfortable European standard of living. To Jews the world over, Israel became a source of pride for its democratic institutions and military prowess. They invested heavily in its cultural, educational, medical, and scientific infrastructure.

The Palestinian minority of 20 percent that remained within Israeli territory became Israeli citizens in a multicultural state with full voting rights. They elected representatives to the Knesset, Israel's parliament; they enjoyed religious freedom; their language, Arabic, had official status; and their children were educated in Arabic-language schools. Yet, many of their Jewish compatriots and government officials suspected their loyalty to the Jewish state, regarding them as the enemy within. Israeli Arabs appreciated the world-class medical care and higher education that were available to them, but were treated as second-class citizens, subject to many forms of discrimination. Along with cohorts from the Occupied Territories, young men from their ranks participated in the *intifada*, the low-intensity warfare that was waged by frustrated young Palestinians in the Occupied Territories against mostly civilian targets, beginning in the 1990s.

Israel's wars

Israelis have never been permitted to enjoy security. As a result, they are compelled to maintain permanent mobilization for defense. Young men and women spend three years in the armed forces and participate in the active reserves until the age of 45. They have fought three wars, in 1956, 1967, and 1973, and confront continuous hostility from

Palestinian militants. In 1967, they defeated the combined armies of their Arab neighbors, seizing the Golan Heights from Syria, the Gaza Strip and Sinai peninsula from Egypt, and the West Bank and all of Jerusalem from Jordan. In an agreement negotiated in 1978 by the US President, Jimmy Carter, they signed a peace treaty with Egypt, returning the territories acquired from Egypt except for Gaza.[23] The treaty was, however, unpopular on the Egyptian streets. Egypt's President, Anwar Sadat, who had signed the treaty and established diplomatic relations with Israel, was regarded as a traitor to the Arab cause. He was later assassinated by Islamist members of his bodyguard.

On the occupied West Bank and Gaza, Israel's government has tolerated and in many cases actually sponsored settlements by religious zealots who regard the West Bank as part of the biblical Jewish patrimony that must be reclaimed for Israel by occupying the land. Other Israelis have been attracted to the settlements by government-subsidized, low-cost housing. The UN and most of its member states regard these settlements as illegal under international law. The West Bank is now honeycombed with expanding Jewish settlements, much of the land requisitioned from Palestinian owners. These settlements are connected to Israel by a network of roads bypassing Palestinian population centers and protected by Israel's armed forces. These settlements greatly complicate prospects for an eventual accord with the Palestinians. Israel is constructing a high 436-mile-long "security wall" intended as a barrier between Israel plus its contiguous settlements and Palestinian territory, intending, thereby, to prevent infiltration by terrorists. To many Palestinians, this wall has become another symbol of their oppression.

The endless conflict

Through diplomatic backchannels orchestrated by Norway's Foreign Office, the PLO under Arafat and Israel under its Prime Minister, Yitzchak Rabin, signed the Oslo Accords in 1993, providing mutual recognition. These contemplated an eventual two-state solution: Palestine including the West Bank and Gaza; Israel in its pre-1967 boundaries, plus the contiguous West Bank settlements. Many critical issues remain unresolved, including the right of displaced Palestinians to return to their former homes in Israel, the fate of Jerusalem – which Israelis regard as their permanent, indivisible capital, but which Palestinians also claim as their capital – and the precise boundaries of the two prospective neighbors. As a result of these preliminary accords, however, Israel broke out of its previous isolation from Arab and non-aligned states. Jordan recognized Israel, as did China and India. A young Jewish religious fanatic assassinated Rabin, who had agreed to the establishment of a Palestinian Authority on the Occupied Territories as a prelude to a negotiated two-state resolution of the conflict.[24]

This hopeful beginning has not, however, brought peace to Israel. A substantial bloc of Israel's voters, activated by religious or security concerns, rejects any limitation on settlements and any reversion of the Occupied Territories; a large and militant faction of Palestinians likewise rejects any accord with Israel. As Israel withdrew its settlers and armed forces from Gaza in 2005, Hamas seized control. In an election in 2006, Hamas won a majority of seats in the Palestinian parliament, though the more moderate Fatah maintained the Presidency and control of the West Bank. Prodded by the US and the Europeans, Israel and Fatah continue sporadic negotiation, but have yet to address the main issues of contention.

On May 14, 2008, Israel celebrated the sixtieth anniversary of its independence. Zionists began as a precarious settler diaspora, convinced that it was reclaiming its heritage, the land promised by God to its ancestors, and providing a refuge for oppressed members of its people living by sufferance as minorities in foreign lands. The non-Jewish inhabitants of that land could leave and join fellow Arabs in their underpopulated neighboring states or remain a minority that would be treated generously and respectfully and benefit from higher living standards in Israel. But many of these inhabitants, especially those in the Occupied Territories, are unwilling to accept the Israeli presence. With support from fellow Arabs and Muslims, young men from the territories have mounted armed resistance and low-intensity attacks, including suicide bombings, against Israeli targets, civilian as well as military. In their propaganda, they attempt to delegitimize Israel as a racist oppressor and an example of latter-day western colonialism. Israeli security forces retaliate with harsh assaults against suspected targets, imprisonment of suspected terrorists, and population controls that inflict daily hardships on Palestinians and prevent Palestinian workers in the Occupied Territories from reaching their jobs in Israel. Instead, Israel has recruited workers from eastern Europe and east Asia for construction jobs, agricultural labor, and other low-skill jobs formerly performed by Palestinians. The effects of these measures are to further impoverish and embitter Palestinians in the Occupied Territories.

A two-state solution?

How Israel's Arab minority value their Israeli citizenship can be illustrated by the following incident. In November 2007, Israeli government sources floated a proposal that a strip of land inhabited by 200,000 Palestinians, including the city of Umm el Fahm, with its 40,000-strong Muslim population, be transferred to the future Palestinian state, in exchange for a strip of West Bank territory inhabited by Jews. They would not be uprooted, but would remain in their homes and be transferred peacefully from alien Jewish rule to Palestinian-Muslim jurisdiction. This proposal was indignantly rejected by spokespersons for the area's residents. They explained that as Israeli citizens, they could not be shifted about without their consent, and they preferred to remain Israelis. They desired, however, that Israel cease to be a Jewish state. Instead, it should become a state for all its citizens. They should enjoy equal status, equal rights, and equal opportunities, and all religions should be equally respected.[25] This would be unacceptable to Israel, as it would signal the defeat of Zionism, the demise of the Jewish state.

Even if Israel and the Fatah faction of Palestinians should eventually agree on the details of a two-state solution, a substantial segment among Palestinians, with considerable foreign support, would continue their struggle by violent means. They would be matched by a similar faction of uncompromising Israeli extremists who insist that Israel must retain every inch of the Occupied Territories, their promised land. Meantime, Israel's principle diplomatic support comes from the United States government which, since 1967, has provided generous economic assistance and high-tech equipment to Israel's formidable military machine. The Jewish diaspora in the United States, passionately committed to Israel's survival, has cobbled together a formidable political coalition, including Protestant evangelicals. They pressure the US government, its executive agencies and its Congress, to provide unquestioning diplomatic and material support to Israel.

A normal nation?

Israel's settler diaspora has successfully absorbed immigrants from many lands. From the ashes of the European Holocaust, on the land hallowed by its ancestors, it has built a modern, Hebrew-speaking nation with a vibrant democratic government, a powerful military presence, world-class educational, medical, and cultural institutions, and an industrial structure that enables its people to prosper economically. After centuries of exile and wandering, the Zionist dream has been realized: the Jewish nation now manages its own affairs on its own land. It has achieved the Zionist goal of creating a "normal" nation with its share of criminals and prostitutes, as well as scientists and musicians, and its internal conflicts between religious and secular factions, and between doves who favor accommodation with its Palestinian neighbors, and hawks who oppose any concessions. It is handicapped by a dysfunctional political system, a large and expanding gap between rich and poor, and an increasingly alienated Palestinian minority.

And it has yet to enjoy the blessings of security and peace. In recent years emigration from Israel has exceeded immigration. In 2007, for example, 20,000 Israelis emigrated, the majority to the United States and Germany. Israeli emigrants living abroad now exceed 100,000. The reasons given for emigration are to escape from the tensions involved in Israel's precarious security situation and the enhanced professional and business opportunities available in the US and Europe. There have been reports that as many as 25 percent of Israelis are considering emigration, indicating a troublesome morale problem in this settler diaspora.

Its Arab and Muslim enemies are confident that time is on their side. With the assistance of sympathizers and *jihadists* from Arab and Muslim countries, they are mobilizing for conflict. Just as the infidel medieval Crusader Kingdom of Jerusalem a thousand years ago, after ruling for a century, was finally defeated and liquidated by Muslim forces under their hero, Salah a'Din, so the Zionist invaders of this Muslim land will eventually be defeated and eliminated. The fate of this twentieth-century settler diaspora, they firmly believe, is sealed.

3d. Ukrainians in Canada

Of the 59 million Ukrainians during the mid-1990s, 22 million, more than a third, lived in the diaspora outside the homeland in eastern Europe. A million resided in Canada.[26]

Three waves

Ukrainians arrived in Canada in three waves. The pre-World War I cohort, by far the largest, consisted mainly of land-hungry peasants attracted to Canada by reports of its generous homesteading incentives in its vast, underpopulated prairie provinces, Manitoba, Saskatchewan, and Alberta. Winnipeg in Manitoba became the cultural hub of Ukrainian settlement in North America. They settled in blocs that enabled them to reproduce, in their diaspora, the familiar religious, social, and economic organization of their homeland, among them cooperatives and credit unions. Most of them came from Galicia, at that time part of the multiethnic Hapsburg Empire. (The eastern half of Ukrainia at that time was ruled by Tsarist Russia.) Ukrainians in Canada maintained close relations with families in the homeland. Their religious leaders emphasized the importance of culture and language maintenance in their host country. Given the relative isolation of their settlements, this appeared to be possible, especially when they succeeded until World War I in securing government-financed bilingual schooling in Manitoba. About 80,000, a third of the original emigrants, trickled back to their homeland. In addition to pioneering farming under the harsh conditions of the prairies, Ukrainian immigrants labored on railway construction and maintenance crews to earn cash income for their families.

Canada, at that time, was part of the British Empire. Its English and Scottish establishment celebrated the virtues of the English-speaking Protestant "race." Ukrainian immigrants, like other eastern and southern Europeans, were tolerated for their economic contributions, but despised for their foreign ways. Establishment spokesmen were fearful that Ukrainian immigrants could never qualify as true Canadians, could never be assimilated into the Anglo-Canadian mainstream. They placed high priority on "Canadianizing" immigrants as soon as possible. Canadianization meant acculturation to the English language and British-Protestant lifestyles. During the hysteria of World War I, while Canada joined the motherland at war with Austria-Hungary, 8,500 Ukrainian-Canadian men were interned in concentration camps as enemy aliens and employed at uncompensated hard labor on infrastructure projects.[27] Others anglicized their names in order to appear less foreign.

The second wave of Ukrainians reached Canada in the late 1920s and early 1930s. They were mostly unskilled peasants who found themselves in unfriendly Polish, Czech, and Rumanian territory as a result of the Versailles settlement, which dismembered the Hapsburg Empire. Most of them settled in Manitoba near Winnipeg, but others formed communities as factory workers in and near Toronto.

The third wave arrived after World War II. The Ukrainian homeland had sustained heavy losses as a result of the Nazi invasion, followed by the Soviet counterattack. An estimated 5.3 million Ukrainians, mostly civilians, perished.[28] The economic infrastructure was totally destroyed. Ukrainians suffered greater damage, disruption, and displacement than any other European people. A quarter-million who had fled the war zone or had cooperated with the Germans in order to resist Soviet communism ended the war as inmates of displaced persons camps. Most were forcibly repatriated to the victorious Soviet Union. Some 40,000 succeeded in gaining admission to Canada, the majority settling in the Toronto area. Several had been professionally trained. They proceeded in short order to assume leadership roles in Ukrainian-Canadian cultural institutions. They were militantly anti-Soviet, condemning its campaigns of collective farming, cultural Russification, persecution of religion, and other human rights abuses.

The Ukrainian-Canadian Congress

Like many diaspora communities, Ukrainians in Canada attempt to sustain a common collective identity and speak through their umbrella organization, the Ukrainian-Canadian Congress. Beneath the umbrella, however, is a complex organizational structure, reflecting numerous cleavages within the Ukrainian diaspora.[29] Their religious life is split between adherents of the Roman Catholic and the Eastern Orthodox churches. Within the second wave, conflict raged, at times violently, between leftists and nationalists. Leftists, centered in Winnipeg, regarded the Soviet Union as a workers' paradise, deserving of sympathy and support by all members of the working class. Nationalists detested it as an oppressive prison, attempting to destroy the Ukrainian nation. They pointed to forced collectivization, the catastrophic man-made famine of 1932–33, the campaign of Russification, and the pillaging of churches as evidence of Stalin's hostility to the Ukrainian people. Leftists accused the nationalists of flirting with Nazi Germany to weaken the Soviet homeland.

Successful Canadianization

Until World War II, mainstream Canadians continued to regard Ukrainians skeptically as a foreign minority that was in Canada, but not yet Canadian. During the war, however, Ukrainian-Canadians enlisted in the armed forces in large numbers. As second- and third-generation residents, they had acculturated to Anglophone Canada and had become fluent English speakers, indistinguishable in appearance, behavior, and speech from other Canadians. Their wartime performance helped to eliminate the remaining prejudices toward Canadians of Ukrainian origin and ushered in their acceptance as fully fledged Canadians. They now participate actively in all the mainstream Anglo-Canadian institutions on a non-discriminatory basis. As evidence of their new-found confidence, Dr Jaroslav Rudnyckyj, the Manitoba member of the Royal Commission on Bilingualism and Biculturalism,[30] promoted the acceptance of Ukrainian, unsuccessfully as it turned out, as an official language of the government of Canada. Since there are more Ukrainian than French speakers in the prairie provinces, he argued, Ukrainian deserved to be recognized as an official language.

The decades after World War II witnessed two contrary developments within the Ukrainian-Canadian fold. The first was the process of rapid assimilation among those born and reared in Canada. They regarded themselves as 100 percent Canadian and were so regarded by fellow Canadians. Their Ukrainian roots, its language, culture and lifestyle, had less and less significance in their daily lives. Educated to the average Anglo-Canadian level, they joined the middle class, moving out of their parents' rural ethnic enclaves and into mainstream urban neighborhoods, marrying in many cases outside their ethnic community. They attained important, prestigious posts in national and provincial governments, including Governor General of Canada, Premiers of Manitoba and Saskatchewan, Justices of the Supreme Court, and numerous elected memberships in Canada's national and provincial parliaments. Elder statesmen have begun to question whether the Ukrainian diaspora will be able to survive these assimilationist pressures, especially in the absence of fresh recruits. In the face of an open opportunity structure, what incentives were available to the upcoming generation to retain and cherish their ethnic heritage?

During the 75 years of Soviet rule, the small coterie of intellectuals within the diaspora believed it was their mission and their responsibility to retain Ukrainian culture, while it was being systematically suppressed in the homeland by Russification. This is not a unique role for diasporas. The Tibetan diaspora in India and the United States has assumed that same responsibility. In 1971, Ukrainian-Canadians greeted with favor the multicultural initiative of Prime Minister Trudeau: financial assistance from the government of Canada to Ukrainian cultural institutions provided additional means and a further incentive to maintain their inherited culture and thus to fulfill their responsibility, while those in the homeland were unable to do so. Hopefully, Canada's multicultural program would enable Ukrainians to flourish as a component of their nation's cultural mosaic.

But, despite generous government support for Canada's Ukrainian cultural institutions, after more than three decades of official multiculturalism, it clearly has not reversed or even retarded the appeal of the mainstream to young Ukrainian-Canadians.

War criminals?

More effective in mobilizing and sustaining the Ukrainian diaspora have been charges levied against several fellow Ukrainians of virulent anti-Semitism and active complicity in the Nazi crimes against humanity, especially the wartime genocide against European Jews. A number of these war criminals were believed to have found their way to North America after the defeat of the Germans. Responding to charges that Canada might be harboring war criminals, in 1985 Ottawa activated a Commission of Inquiry into Alleged War Criminals in Canada. The commission identified 200 individuals for further inquiry as possible offenders. The most celebrated case, however, arose across the border in the United States. There, John Demjanjuk, an elderly retired auto worker in Michigan, was accused of numerous instances of sadistic brutalization of inmates while serving as a guard at the Treblinka concentration camp. He was arrested by the US government and found to have concealed information about his Nazi background at the time of his naturalization. His US citizenship was revoked and he was deported to Israel for trial on charges of crimes against humanity. After a two-year trial, he was convicted by the Israeli court and sentenced to death, but his conviction was overturned by a higher court in Israel. He was eventually returned to the United States, where his citizenship was restored.

The Demjanjuk and several similar cases mobilized the Ukrainian diaspora in Canada, concerned to defend their collective reputation against what they were convinced were false charges of anti-Semitism, pro-Nazi sympathies, and participation in war crimes; and to protest the unwarranted persecution and brutal victimization of elderly fellow Ukrainians, such as John Demjanjuk. The war crimes accusation brought the organized Ukrainian diaspora into conflict with Canada's Jewish diaspora, which was urging the government of Canada to proceed more actively against war criminals residing in their country.[31] The organized Jewish community opposed the effort of the Ukrainian diaspora to have the Soviet-induced famine of 1932–33 declared a genocide; Ukrainians, in turn, successfully opposed a campaign by the Jewish community to have a section of the War Memorial Building in Ottawa devoted to the Holocaust.

Victimization and defense

The sense of victimization is a theme that tends to mobilize and consolidate the solidarity of diasporas long after the events themselves and long after they have lost other grounds for survival as distinct communities. Among Ukrainians, there are several brutal memories of disasters inflicted within living memory on their ancestors. These include the imposition by Stalin in 1929–30 of collective agriculture, resulting in the destruction of their cherished way of life. It was followed by the famine of 1932–33, caused by the forced delivery of grain to the Soviet state, leading to the starvation of more than a million Ukrainian peasants. These were followed in short order by World War II, when the German invasion and occupation of their homeland and the Soviet counterattack left 6.8 million of their countrymen dead, their economy in shambles, and their survivors accused of collective anti-Semitism and participation in Nazi war crimes. The accumulated Ukrainian casualties of these tragedies totaled half the male and a quarter of the female population of their devastated homeland. During the postwar economic recovery, the survivors were subject to intensive Russification and persecution of their religion. Adding insult to injury, in June 1986 the Chernobyl nuclear facility leaked deadly radioactive mist over large areas of Ukraine, claiming thousands of victims who overwhelmed the area's hospital and relief facilities. The Canadian diaspora responded promptly with medical supplies, laboratory facilities, and material relief to assist the victims.

Then, more recently, having rebuilt their lives in North America, innocent members of the diaspora and, by inference, all Ukrainians were being falsely accused and branded as war criminals. Self-respecting Ukrainians in the diaspora felt it a matter of personal obligation and honor to defend the good name of their community and rally to the aid of fellow Ukrainians who faced official prosecution and deportation. Victimization and defense are two themes that can sustain the cohesion of diaspora communities, including members who have integrated into the mainstream of their host country.

This pattern of victimization, the memory and more recent events that impugn the honor of their people, helped to maintain identification with and attachment to the diaspora community, even among Ukrainian-Canadians who have lost the language and blended into the Anglo-Canadian mainstream and its way of life. At this point it is uncertain whether memories of collective victimization, plus pride in the newly independent Ukrainian state, will suffice to overcome the powerful assimilationist pressures of Canada's open opportunity structure. Will Canada's Ukrainian diaspora community, more than 90 percent Canada born and reared, manage to maintain itself through the twenty-first century; or will it close this chapter of Ukrainian history?

The diaspora and independent Ukraine[32]

In June 1991, the Soviet Union suddenly and unexpectedly imploded. From its collapse, each of its constituent republics, including the Ukrainian Federated Socialist Republic, gained its independence. The long-sought goal of Ukrainian patriots, within the homeland and in the diaspora, was suddenly realized, entirely peacefully. However, the euphoria lasted only a short time. It soon became apparent that independence yielded economic disaster for the Ukrainian people. Its economy, including sources of supply for its archaic, inefficient industries and markets for its products, had been tightly integrated into the now defunct, centrally planned Soviet economy.

Independence created total economic disruption. Large-scale unemployment, high inflation, widespread want and demoralization accompanied the early years of independence. Criminal syndicates with ties to ex-Communist government officials emerged to control the distribution of scarce supplies. As families stopped having children, population within the republic began to decline. Though emigration was difficult, due to restrictions imposed by most prospective host governments, a small number found ways to leave, some legally, many illegally, seeking opportunities to earn decent livelihoods in western Europe and North America. Some impoverished families yielded their children for adoption by eager North American and European couples. Some young women, promised alluring jobs in the West, ended up as sweatshop laborers, sex slaves, or domestic servants.

The number of new arrivals to Canada has been sufficient to constitute a fourth wave. After 75 years of near total separation, the reunion of diaspora and homeland came as somewhat of a shock. Visitors to the homeland, eager to renew contact with families and former communities, soon discovered the chasm between themselves, products of Canada's affluent and democratic environment, and those who had endured nearly a century of privation and Russification under Soviet rule. The modest number who reached Canada proved in most cases to be disappointments, even embarrassments, to members of the established diaspora. Their manners and behavior were judged to be uncouth, their work ethic underdeveloped, they expected handouts from government, and some spoke only Russian or crude Russian-Ukrainian dialects.

The diaspora in Canada, as well as in the United States, did what it could to assist fellow Ukrainians in the independent homeland. A handful actually returned to take up residence and contribute technical skills and business acumen learned in the West to their homeland's renewal as a capitalist, market economy and democratic polity. Since the government of Ukraine refused to recognize dual citizenship, while the returnees declined to abandon their Canadian passports, they remained visitors to their homeland. A stifling bureaucracy blocked the establishment of western-style businesses. Money and supplies were contributed in Canada to assist families and needy communities and to support their economic recovery. Student exchanges were arranged, financed, and implemented. Members of the remaining factions in the diaspora provided financial aid and moral support to competing political parties in the homeland.

Activist members of Canada's Ukrainian diaspora urged their counterparts in the United States to pressure the US government to support the candidacy of Viktor Yuschenko and his Orange Revolution against Russian-supported Viktor Yanukovich in the presidential election of December 2006. Despite widespread voter fraud in favor of his opponent, Yuschenko won the election. As most members of the diaspora in Canada hailed originally from the western region of their country, formerly held by Austria-Hungary, they strongly favored Yuschenko, whose base of support was in the west and who advocated closer relations with the European Union and the United States. His opponent's base was in the eastern Trans-dnestrian region, formerly ruled by Tsarist Russia and currently home to a large Russian minority. He was perceived as Russian President Putin's candidate, especially after Putin's ham-handed intervention on his behalf.

The independent homeland is a source of pride to Ukrainians everywhere, the fulfillment of their long-sought dream. Fortunately, its continued existence is in no way threatened. Unlike Israel and Armenia, whose defense and very survival seem to require the nurturing vigilance and assistance of their diasporas, independent Ukraine can get along without the patronage of its diaspora. The members of the diaspora, in turn, have not developed the same degree of commitment to their homeland as their Jewish and Armenian counterparts. The emergence of their ancestral homeland as a sovereign member of the community of nations, and the sight of its flag fluttering over the embassy in Ottawa and the United Nations Headquarters in New York, have not retarded the gradual assimilation of Canada-born members of the Ukrainian diaspora into the Anglo-Canadian mainstream.[33]

3e. The "Russian" diaspora in Israel

Except for its 20 percent Arab minority, Israel is a nation of recent arrivals. When it achieved statehood in 1948, its Jewish population barely reached 600,000. Six decades later, due to immigration, it had swollen to 5.5 million. In 2000, 40 percent of Israelis were first-generation immigrants. Government policy emphasized "immigrant absorption" – rapid assimilation into the Hebrew-speaking mainstream.

The Russians arrived in two waves. The 1970s immigrants, about 100,000, were mainly "refuseniks," committed Zionists, several of whom had served prison terms for their forbidden Zionist speech and writings. They were very reluctantly permitted by the Soviet authorities to leave the country under pressure from the western powers in fulfillment of provisions of the 1975 Helsinki agreements.[34] These European immigrants accommodated readily to Israel's assimilationist policy, learning Hebrew eagerly, participating in its institutions, and soon joining the Israeli-Jewish melting pot.

Why did they come to Israel?

The much larger 1990s wave, totaling about 900,000, nearly 20 percent of Israel's population, came to Israel not in most cases as Zionists, but for pragmatic reasons following the collapse and breakup of the Soviet Union. They left Russia, Ukraine, and the newly independent Baltic, Caucasus, and central Asian states to escape their severely depressed economies or nationalist anti-Semitism and attain a better life for themselves and their children. Many would have preferred to begin their new lives in the United States, Canada, or even Germany, but as these doors were closed to them, they decided to make do with Israel. As many as 25 percent were non-Jews, most with Jewish spouses, though some had no Jewish connections at all.[35] They were a heterogeneous population, from the diverse areas of the defunct Soviet Empire, ranging from urbanized St Petersburg and Moscow sophisticates to more traditional, less cultivated petty traders and craftsmen from Georgia and Uzbekistan. Most were secular, religiously non-observant, with little exposure to Judaism, Jewish culture, or Zionist ideology, and only faint memories of their Jewish origins. What they had in common were the Russian language, an intense pride in and commitment to Russian culture, plus a belief in the superiority of their Russian cultural heritage to what they considered the less developed, much less sophisticated, and parochial Middle Eastern Hebrew culture they encountered in Israel.

Previous waves of Jewish immigrants had been carefully and paternalistically guided and supervised from their arrival through language training, housing, settlement selection, and occupational "absorption" into Israeli society. This policy had been implemented with displaced persons, the remnant of eastern European Jewry after the Holocaust, who finally found refuge in Israel immediately after independence in 1948; and shortly thereafter, with the large "Sephardic" migration, Mitzrachim (Easterners) from the Mediterranean basin and the Middle East. These and other new arrivals had been guided to "development towns," away from the crowded urban centers, with the intention of distributing Israel's population throughout its territory for both economic and security reasons. However, the right-wing government in power in the early 1990s, with its neo-liberal skepticism about government and its faith in market processes, allowed the arriving Russians to make their own settlement, housing, and occupational choices. As no specific preparations had been made to receive them, this unexpected tidal wave of Russians soon overwhelmed the social services of the Jewish Agency, responsible for the reception of immigrants, as well as the Israeli bureaucracy, local non-government organizations, and available housing in the largest cities, Haifa, Tel Aviv, and Jerusalem, where the majority, former urban dwellers, chose to locate.

Russians, an entrepreneurial diaspora

For the most part, the Russians, unlike their Sephardic predecessors, were an educated, professional group, doctors, engineers, scientists, musicians, academic teachers, and researchers. They soon found that the small Israeli labor market was unable to absorb them in their previous high-status occupations. Consequently, many were forced to accept sub-professional or even menial jobs; in 1992, a third were unemployed, with damaging effects on their morale and self-esteem.[36] Some suffered discrimination due to the refusal of veteran Israelis to honor their Soviet professional credentials, combined with their inability to work in Hebrew. Notwithstanding their professional backgrounds, some ventured successfully into businesses that catered initially to the many needs of their immigrant compatriots. More than 50,000 chose to return to Russia, unwilling to tolerate the disquieting security problems that confront most Israelis, and disappointed at the limited professional opportunities in Israel's small-scale, crowded and parochial economy.

Like most diaspora communities, the Russians concentrated in residential enclaves. There they could lead their lives in the Russian language in a familiar environment. Shops, restaurants and cafés featuring Russian cuisine (including non-kosher pork sausages), entertainment facilities (including Russian-language radio and television channels), bookstores, garages, travel agencies, newspapers, and magazines sprang up, advertising their many products and services in bold Cyrillic lettering. The Russians never regarded themselves as a minority community. Under Israel's law of return, as Jews putatively returning to their ancient homeland, they attained full citizenship immediately upon arrival. Moreover, as secular Europeans, they identified with Ashkenazim, Jews of European origin, whose parents had been the pioneer settlers, founders of the state and builders of its main institutions. Ashkenazim continued to monopolize elite positions in the military, educational, scientific, governmental, judicial, economic, and professional institutions of Israeli society. Russians formed their own political parties that won seats in the Knesset, Israel's parliament, and participated actively in national and local politics. As an important voting bloc, they were courted by all the secular parties.

They allied in Israel's coalition politics with the secular, hard-line anti-Arab forces represented mainly by the right-wing Likud party. They were repelled by the Labor Party, which they regarded as socialist, similar in too many respects to the discredited Communists in their former homeland.

Their uncompromising xenophobia toward Arabs has complicated hope for a two-state compromise solution to the Israeli–Palestinian predicament. While most learned sufficient Hebrew to interact with the mainstream economy and government, among themselves, in their homes and communities, their language remained Russian and their social networks were confined to fellow Russians. Only after they felt comfortable with their Hebrew and began to interact professionally with veteran Israelis did some of the younger immigrants begin to venture outside their diaspora cocoon. Their political identity was Israeli; their social identity remained Russian. They maintained a dual or hybrid identity.[37]

A transnational existence

Because of inexpensive and efficient communications and transportation, many Russians in Israel maintain active telephone and e-mail contact with relatives, friends, and business associates in the cities of the former Soviet Union. Some have even held on to their former apartments. Visits to their former homeland are common. In effect, they lead transnational existences, including dual citizenship, living and participating in their former countries as well as in Israel. In addition to the 50,000 who have returned to Russia, others await the opportunity to move on to the United States or Canada.

The immigrant flow from the former Soviet Union diminished and virtually ceased after 1995. Despite their difficult and often painful transition and adjustment, by the end of the 1990s their unemployment rate had declined to about 10 percent, mostly elderly individuals. The expanding Israeli economy increasingly found room for the Russian immigrants in positions compatible with their professional status and expectations. The highly educated scientists and engineers among them contributed significantly to Israel's economic surge in the 1990s as innovators, producers, and exporters of high-tech services and manufactured items. They had attained higher standards of living in Israel's expanding economy than would have been available in the stagnant economies of Russia and the other successor states of the former Soviet Union.

After first settling in the three major conurbations, the Russians have gradually spread out, establishing themselves also in Israel's secondary cities, such as Hadera, Karmiel, Upper Nazareth, and Be'er Sheba. Politically and economically, many have joined Israel's mainstream. Culturally and socially, however, the first-generation Russian immigrants maintain their collective identity and cultural pride, refusing to be absorbed into the Hebrew-speaking mainstream. This has generated tensions among veteran Israelis, as it violates the Zionist creed of a single Jewish nation and a single Hebrew culture. They express annoyance and object to hearing Russian spoken in public places.[38]

Ashkenazic, Sephardic, and orthodox reception

The large Russian influx was greeted with enthusiasm in Ashkenazic circles, for it strengthened their position in Israeli politics as well as the Jewish presence in their homeland. It was received more guardedly by many Sephardim, who retain bitter memories of their early days in Israel when they or their parents were patronized by the Ashkenazic establishment, their culture demeaned, and their economic prospects blunted by forced location in remote "development towns." As petty traders and craftsmen, Sephardic Jews were unacquainted with the European Zionist ideology of pioneering return to the soil, and were unequipped for participation in the agricultural settlements to which they were assigned. They sensed that they might suffer discrimination in favor of the new arrivals in competition for scarce housing, jobs, and government assistance.

Similarly, the orthodox establishment suspected as many as 25 percent of the new arrivals of being non-Jews (whose mothers were not Jewish), and thus not entitled to acceptance as genuine Israelis. By strengthening the secular element in Israeli politics, they jeopardized the ability of orthodox politicians to extract subsidies from the national budget for their educational institutions and the housing and subsistence of their large families. The refusal of the rabbinate, who are alone authorized to conduct marriages, grant divorces, and preside at Jewish burials, to perform these rituals for Israeli citizens whom they judge to be non-Jews has caused intense and highly publicized heartache and resentment among Russian immigrants as well as other Israelis. Their loved ones cannot be buried in Jewish cemeteries and they must leave the country to marry or secure divorces. They regard themselves as victims of a medieval cabal that is tolerated for political reasons by the Israeli government. These many internal tensions are, however, countered by their mutual appreciation of the imperative need for solidarity in the face of Israel's precarious security situation, the sense that their nation remains under siege by unrelenting Arab and Muslim enemies.

Political, economic, and social adjustment

The story of the Russians in Israel is, of course, ongoing and incomplete. The longer-term impact of this large, mainly professional, entrepreneurial diaspora's influx on Israel's mainstream culture remains to be seen. As summarized by the sociologist, Al-Haj, at the end of the 1990s:

> On the whole we found that the 1990s immigrants from the FSU form a distinct group, with strong social and cultural borders, with regard to their residential patterns, social networks, and social relations with the host society. Immigrants are satisfied about their absorption in Israel, although their social adjustment lags behind their material adaptation. However, immigrants perceive themselves as having a more positive influence on Israeli society than it has on them and have already crystallized their social location vis-à-vis other groups in Israel.[39]

The second generation, born and educated in Israel, fluent in Hebrew, with three years of training and experience in the army, one of the nation's most effective socializing agencies, have yet to make their mark. Will they, like second-generation north African youth in France, reject and turn their backs on

Israel's assimilationist expectations? Will they demand acceptance as a separate cultural community, but with full political
rights in a multicultural state, unlike the large Arab community that has been relegated to second-class citizenship? Or,
as seems more likely, will they agree, like Thailand's Chinese
youth, to participate as individuals and be absorbed into
Israel's Hebrew-speaking cultural and social mainstream?

Readers are likely to note that in many respects the adjustment of the Russians in Israel has been similar to the
experience of other entrepreneurial/professional diasporas.
But, unlike the Chinese diaspora in southeast Asia, they do
not constitute a middleman minority, since they have joined
a society already richly stocked with entrepreneurs and professionals. In addition, they are already citizens and, as
Europeans by background and culture, they identify and
expect to be regarded as Ashkenazim, who occupy the elite
stratum of Israeli society. The opportunity structure in Israel
offers them few barriers to admission, meritocratic success,
and eventual integration. In his 1999 survey, Al-Haj reported
that, notwithstanding their feeling of rejection by many
veteran Israelis, 80 percent were satisfied with their absorption into Israeli society; 75 percent already owned their own
apartments and one-third of Israel's licensed medical doctors
were immigrants from the former Soviet Union.[40]

It appears unlikely that the immigrant generation will
abandon their strong commitment to Russian culture. The
main question is whether successive Israel-born generations
of the Russian diaspora will be inclined to accept absorption
into Israel's mainstream, or whether they will insist on retaining and being recognized as a separate cultural minority
within a pluralistic Jewish nation.[41]

3f. Afro-Brazilians, 1531–2008[42]

Afro-Brazilians are an example of a diaspora that has endured
through centuries because of a rigid, exclusionary opportunity structure in its host country.

Africans have been in Brazil in large numbers for nearly five centuries. 3.5 million Africans were transported to Brazil to provide slave labor for their Portuguese masters, serving as the labor force in the mines, cane fields, and sugar mills. At the time that slavery was finally abolished in 1888, they constituted a majority of the population. In order to raise the "quality" of their human capital, Brazil's elites implemented a policy of population "whitening." They subsidized the immigration of Europeans and encouraged miscegenation, in the belief that the superior white element in the blood of mixed-race individuals would gradually improve its quality.[43] At the turn of the present century, an estimated 45 percent of Brazilians – 80 million of Brazil's 170 million – are identified as Black (*preto*) or Mulatto (*pardo*), while a large number who pass as White possess some African genetic heritage. Blacks are present in all the regions of this vast country, but are most numerous in the northeast and the southeast.

The myth of racial democracy

Brazil's elites have consistently cultivated the myth of racial democracy. There are not and have never been Jim Crow laws in their country, no legally sanctioned or mandated racial discrimination. Legally, all Brazilian citizens are equal before the law, enjoy the same opportunities, and are vested with the same responsibilities. But the facts belie this fiction.[44] Brazilians display an acute sensitivity to skin color. Individuals are identified and evaluated according to the shade of their pigmentation; the lighter, the better. In a United Nations-sponsored survey in 1991, Brazilian respondents employed more than a hundred shades of color to describe themselves and to differentiate themselves from Blacks.[45] In reality, Brazilian society is highly stratified. By every social indicator of income, educational achievement, life expectancy, infant mortality, housing, living conditions, and prestige, Afro-Brazilians occupy the lowest rungs of the social ladder. Around 90 percent of those in poverty are *preto* or *pardo*. At every level of education, there are substantial income differentials; the higher the level of education, the greater the income disparities between equally qualified Whites and Blacks.[46]

Though they have long since acculturated to the main-stream Portuguese language and values, Afro-Brazilians have been marginalized in every dimension of Brazilian life, except in sports and entertainment, where they excel. Apologists for Brazil's racial "democracy" tirelessly mention the soccer great, Pele, as evidence of the opportunity and recognition available to ambitious persons of color. Though Whites and Blacks mix freely in public places – there are no separate toilets, drinking fountains, or seating arrangements – prejudice and discrimination are endemic, resulting in a pattern of "cordial racism." Blacks are seldom visible in elite circles of government, industry, or academia, or in upper- and middle-class residential neighborhoods.

Stratification patterns

The stratification patterns are perpetuated intergeneration-ally. Because of poverty, absence of role models, and poor educational preparation in substandard public schools, including high dropout rates, as many as 50 percent of the Afro-Brazilian diaspora are believed to be functionally illit-erate. Fewer than 1 percent complete higher education. Unemployment is high, and those who find jobs occupy the less skilled, poorly paid positions in government agencies and private firms, and for women, domestic service. Thus, income inequality in Brazil is among the world's highest; average per capita income of Blacks is less than half that of Whites. Most landless laborers in rural Brazil, descendants of former slaves, especially in the northeast, are Blacks – as are the great majority of inhabitants of the notorious, crime-ridden *favellas*, sprawling slum settlements on the outskirts of major cities.[47]

Young Black males, routinely harassed by the police, are the principal preoccupation of the criminal justice system, resulting in a heavy concentration of young Black males in overcrowded prisons.[48] In 1992, protests and riots in the infamous Carandiru penitentiary resulted in the massacre of 111 inmates, mostly Black.[49] The occasional Black who manages to achieve a good education is nevertheless likely to encounter exclusion or discrimination and lower compensation in the professional and managerial labor market. Incomes for persons of African heritage at all levels of educational achievement, including university graduates, are significantly lower than for their White counterparts. Nevertheless, money is believed to "whiten"; occupational success enables dark-skinned individuals to be perceived as near-White!

Though Africans have been in Brazil for half a millennium, and have contributed significantly to its mainstream culture, especially to music, cuisine, literature, and theatre, they remain an identifiable marginalized community. In this sense, the Afro-Brazilian diaspora has yet to be incorporated into the Brazilian mainstream. Informal exclusion and discrimination coexist with substantial racial mixing and miscegenation. The latter occurs, however, on an intra-class basis between poor Whites and persons of color who live in residentially mixed neighborhoods and share similar patterns of poverty. Miscegenation in middle- and upper-class circles remains rare. Brazil's racial inequalities are institutionalized by three mechanisms: 1) *hyper-inequality* of wealth and income, 2) a *discriminatory glass ceiling* that inhibits upward mobility for persons of color, and 3) a *racist culture* that correlates skin color with inherent inferiority.[50]

The 1988 constitution and its aftermath

Brazil's liberal 1988 constitution, enacted after the demise of its brutal, reactionary, and repressive military regime (1964–79/85) criminalizes racial discrimination and racism: "The practice of racism constitutes a crime. . .punishable by imprisonment." This provision has been implemented by legislation that defines and sets penalties for racist and discriminatory practices. Yet, few cases have been adjudicated under these provisions and no one has served prison time for violating the anti-discrimination laws.[51] In practice, they continue to be ignored in the behavior of employers, land-lords, and the police. Most Afro-Brazilians lack the means to initiate legal action against offenders. A Black civil rights movement began only in the 1990s. A large number of non-government organizations (NGOs) have emerged, some domestic, others transnational, devoted to the promotion of human rights, job training, education, and legal advocacy. Their main frustration has been the limited help they receive from their intended beneficiaries.

Despite their tradition of slave revolts during the nine-teenth century, Brazil's Blacks have yet to mobilize politically.[52] Individual Blacks compete for office and are elected at local and state levels, but few succeed in national politics, in part because they lack the financial wherewithal for successful electioneering. The fact is that Blacks seldom vote for fellow Blacks. Their political participation is diffused over several political parties and seldom focuses on specific Black issues. Black activists and their supporters prefer to avoid conflict on racial themes, complying with the prevail-ing leftist Latin-American tendency to define their inequality as a class-based, rather than a race-based phenomenon. Cultural themes that might focus Black self-organization tend to be appropriated and taken over by mainstream popular culture.

Efforts to mobilize Blacks for political action to articulate their distinctive grievances and demands have been continu-ously thwarted, both by the political establishment and by Blacks themselves. The constituent myth of racial democracy has been exploited by the political establishment to brand any suggestion of racial mobilization as subversive of the nation's enlightened, non-racial, and inclusive social order, of creating racial grievances where none had existed and none is justified. Prejudiced attitudes are conceded, but, it is argued, these should be attacked and corrected by education, not by political action. Proposals for affirmative action to increase black participation in higher education and employ-ment have been condemned as reverse discrimination against better-qualified Whites. Low levels of education and occupational status undermine the appeal of Afro-Brazilian candidates for office, even among their potential constituents.[53] Many persist in concentrating on whitening their appearance, so that they might pass for Whites and avoid the prevailing discrimination and stigmatization against people of color. Many Blacks still dream of becoming White.

As far back as 1932 a Black Front was organized by a group of Afro-Brazilian intellectuals in the São Paulo area, the center of the nation's economic life.[54] It urged more rapid assimilation of Blacks into the national mainstream by self-help efforts. While at its peak it claimed 200,000 adherents, it gained little traction in Black circles and was suppressed by the Vargas dictatorship in the 1940s. The aforementioned military regime suppressed all political organizations, including the Black Experimental Theatre, which promoted Black consciousness, raising self-esteem while popularizing Afro-inspired cultural themes. The military resisted any questioning of the myth of racial democracy. It approved the establishment of an Afro-Brazilian Museum that emphasized the nation's unique racial democracy. After the welcome demise of the military regime, a United Negro Movement appeared, assisted by international non-governmental organizations committed to promoting human rights. With its Marxist emphasis on class struggle, it too gained only a small following. It claimed some credit for achieving the anti-racist provisions of the 1988 constitution.

Progress in the 1990s

Afro-Brazilians face the choice of fostering cultural/religious pluralism, emphasizing Black consciousness and their unique Afro-centric traditions, or continuing to struggle for acceptance and integration into the dominant mainstream. The latter strategy has been preferred by the great majority of Afro-Brazilians.

Nevertheless, under pressure from international organizations and human rights agencies, the 1990s witnessed increased

discussion and debate in government and in mainstream publications and opinion circles about public policies to alleviate
the depressed condition of Afro-Brazilians. Multiculturalism
was not seriously considered in a society that emphasizes
nationalism and patriotism, but there were insistent demands
that the anti-discrimination clause in the 1988 constitution
be taken seriously and enforced. During the presidency of
Fernando Henrique Cardoso in the 1990s, a Secretariat of
Human Rights was established in the Federal cabinet, and the
Palmares Cultural Foundation in the Federal Ministry of
Culture promoted Black-oriented cultural activities. During
the 1990s, *Raca Brasil*, the first magazine for Blacks, made its
appearance. Land tenure rights for descendants of escaped
former slaves were finally guaranteed by statute.

In the belief that anti-discrimination measures are necessary
but insufficient to uplift the Black community, proposals for
affirmative action made their hesitant appearance. Yet, when
goals and quotas in employment and university admissions
were proposed, they encountered fierce resistance as reverse
discrimination and subversive of Brazil's enlightened, non-
racial social order. Pressure for affirmative action was reflected
in 2002 in statements by the newly elected, left-of-center
President, Luiz Inacio Lula da Silva (Lula), whose campaign
was supported by lower-income Brazilians, including Afro-
Brazilians. He appointed several persons of color to high
political and judicial positions. In 2003, he established a
Secretariat for Racial Equality, but it suffered from a shortage
of funds and limited enforcement authority. He then proposed
a quota system for university admissions, but this and similar
proposals for affirmative action floundered in Congress, reflecting the resistance of members' middle-class constituents.

Nevertheless, there has been slow, but noticeable progress
during Lula's two-term presidency. The economic position
of Afro-Brazilians has improved somewhat, as the share of
national income accruing to the lowest 50 percent of the
population increased from 9.8 to 11.9 percent.[55] By 2005, 9
percent of the student body at the University of São Paulo,
the nation's most prestigious, were Black.

The largest community of African heritage outside Africa, Afro-Brazilians remain, after nearly five centuries, a marginalized labor diaspora that has yet to be incorporated into the Brazilian national mainstream. Legally, there are no bars to their progress as individuals, but informally they encounter continuing crippling discrimination from a society that assigns status according to color and stereotypes Blacks as congenitally inferior. It relegates them to second-class status because inferiority is believed to be "in their blood."[56] Their poverty breeds intergenerational deprivation, low aspirations, and social delinquency.

Acculturation and elements of the African heritage

Over the centuries, Brazil's African diaspora has long since acculturated to Brazil's mainstream language and lifestyles, and lost touch with families and communities in Africa. Yet, elements of its African heritage have survived and continue to infuse Afro-Brazilians' daily lives, especially in the northeast where they constitute a large majority of the population.[57] *Candomblé*, their religious tradition, is distinctively west African in origin. It is observed and practiced actively by many Afro-Brazilians, and elements of its ceremonies have been appropriated by Brazil's mainstream popular culture. *Capoeira*, a system of African martial arts, has been taken over by the military and police organizations as a national sport and exploited as a tourist attraction. Brazil's mainstream culture, its art, music, theatre, and literature, has incorporated as its own many elements borrowed from the Afro-Brazilian diaspora. *Feijoada*, for example, an African delicacy, has become the favorite national dish.

While Afro-Brazilians have demonstrated their desire to be accepted as equals, they continue to be blocked by an opportunity structure that constrains their admission into the mainstream. Though they constitute a near majority of the population, they are divided by factions and have yet to exhibit collective solidarity or mobilize for political action on their behalf. Will they eventually be inspired by examples of the indigenous communities of Bolivia, Ecuador, and Peru? After centuries of exploitation and neglect, these depressed Andean communities have finally succeeded in mobilizing politically. They demand recognition and respect for their culture by government and by White and Mestizo (mixed Spanish and indigenous) society, more equitable inclusion and participation in mainstream educational and economic institutions, and tangible responses to their individual and collective economic demands.

3g. Palestinians in Kuwait

When Palestinians were uprooted and displaced from their homeland following the defeat of the combined Arab armies in 1948 and again in 1967 and the establishment and consolidation of the state of Israel, they were accepted as citizens only in neighboring Jordan, which had annexed the West Bank and East Jerusalem. Elsewhere in the Arab world, where the refugees had hoped to be received as brothers, they were instead classified as aliens, confined to refugee camps, denied local employment, and supported as dependants by the United Nations Works and Relief Agency (UNWRA).

A conspicuous exception was Kuwait, the Persian Gulf desert sheikhdom. There, the oil boom beginning in the early 1950s created vast wealth and ambitions that overwhelmed the limited human resources of its sparse, undereducated, and underskilled native population.[58] Palestinians at all skill levels, doctors, engineers, teachers, architects, businessmen, as well as skilled craftsmen and unskilled peasants, all were welcome. They soon became the technical and managerial core of the booming Kuwait economy, clearing its path to near instant modernization. The Palestinian diaspora was structured by a dense network of extended family and village associations. These associations furnished supports of all kinds for new arrivals and continued to provide services and emotional stability to its members in their exile homes.

By the 1980s, the hard-working Palestinian diaspora in Kuwait had achieved a comfortable middle class and in many cases an affluent lifestyle, holding key positions in government agencies and state corporations, in the military, and in the private sector. They were accorded the highest status among the several resident ethnic communities in Kuwait's recently assembled, ethnically heterogeneous labor force. They were able to remit substantial funds to relatives who had managed to remain in Israel, the occupied West Bank and Gaza, and in Jordan and the refugee camps in Lebanon and Syria.

Ties to the PLO

They were generous contributors to the Palestine Liberation Organization (PLO), reinforcing their yearning to return one day to their homeland.[59] They raised families and provided amply for their needs. With the acquiescence of the Kuwaiti authorities, a number of the younger immigrants and Kuwait-born sons joined Fatah and participated in its guerilla operations against Israeli and Jewish targets. The PLO office in Kuwait coordinated the activities of the several Palestinian associations and was permitted to levy a 3 percent tax on the incomes of resident Palestinians. The proceeds were used to provide charity to needy Palestinians and to pay school fees for low-income Palestinian students. These included West Bank refugees displaced by the 1967 war, many of whom subsisted in poverty after reaching Kuwait.

Recognizing the value of education for an uprooted and insecure people, Palestinian parents sent many sons and daughters abroad for higher education and professional training in the US, the UK, and the American universities in Cairo and Beirut. Education, they trusted, was the source of human capital that no one could take away from them.

Sufferance: the fate of resident outsiders

A productive and prosperous entrepreneurial diaspora, they were nonetheless insecure because they remained in Kuwait

at the sufferance of its rulers.[60] Victims of defeat and abandonment by Arab governments and by the international
community, they remained exiles, allowed, even encouraged,
to contribute to Kuwait's governance and economy and to
prosper, but excluded from indigenous Kuwaiti society. They
remained powerless politically, denied Kuwaiti citizenship
and the right to participate in politics or hold office. Kuwaiti
citizenship was strictly limited to permanent residents of the
sheikhdom in 1920 and their male progeny.[61] Palestinians
and other guest workers were classified as resident aliens.[62]

The government emphasized the social superiority of
native Kuwaitis over immigrants and was careful to ensure
that all top jobs in government agencies, public corporations,
educational and cultural institutions were reserved for Kuwaiti
citizens.[63] Aliens were not allowed to own land. All private
enterprises were required to have 51 percent Kuwaiti ownership. In the echelons below them, guest workers, more than
half the population, kept the economy running and performed
all the practical managerial, technical, and labor operations.
Kuwaitis assumed a rentier posture, shunning entrepreneurship, hard work, and technical skills. More than 80 percent
were employed by government or government corporations.

Under the policy of Kuwaitization, as more native Kuwaitis
achieved higher education, more senior positions were
reserved for them and denied to guest workers.[64] When a
Kuwaiti and a Palestinian held similar positions, the Kuwaitis
always received a higher salary. Palestinian entrepreneurs
initiating business enterprises were required to find Kuwaiti
"partners" (legally, "sponsors") who shared in the profits,
while Palestinians provided the entrepreneurship and management. This was similar to the Ali-Baba syndrome in
Malaysia, where Chinese (Baba) owned and managed an
enterprise, while the Malay partner (Ali) served as the native
front man and shared in the profits. Nevertheless, so profit-
able were some of these enterprises that several Palestinian
businesspeople became quite wealthy.

In 1985, prior to the Iraqi invasion, the 400,000 Palestinians
comprised between 20 and 25 percent of Kuwait's total

population of just above two million. A mere 4,000 had been permitted over the years to naturalize and become Kuwaiti citizens. The policy of the regime toward guest workers was strictly anti-integrationist. Guest workers, especially Palestinians, were treated courteously, but firmly. There was virtually no social intercourse and no intermarriage. The opportunity structure was thus open to Palestinians on the economic and occupational sides, but on the political and social sides they were kept at arm's length. Many Kuwaitis envied and resented Palestinians, whom they regarded as rich, arrogant foreigners. As integration into Kuwaiti society was not an option for Palestinians, they were destined to remain outsiders.[65] Excluded from Kuwaiti citizenship, they clung to their Palestinian identity and to the dream of eventual return to their homeland and the ultimate victory of the PLO.

The second catastrophe

What Palestinians in Kuwait most feared would disturb their comfortable existence in exile struck suddenly and without warning. On August 2, 1990, Kuwait was invaded by an Iraqi force, its small army was overwhelmed, and its oil installations were torched. Yasir Arafat, Chairman of the PLO, issued a statement in support of the Iraqi invasion and Saddam's plan to annex Kuwait to Iraq as its fifteenth province. Several Palestinians had joined the Iraq invasion force and were so recognized by Kuwaitis. In the wake of the Iraqi invasion, sensing their vulnerability, 200,000, nearly half the Palestinians, left Kuwait hastily, finding refuge in Jordan where the majority were able to reclaim their citizenship. Thus Kuwaitis regarded Palestinians as ingrates and traitors.

Immediately after Kuwait was liberated by the American military in February 1991 and the Kuwaiti regime was restored, it responded by systematically harassing the remaining Palestinians, denying them work permits and access to public services, and prodding them to leave the country. The PLO office was closed. Several thousand Palestinians were imprisoned, suspected of aiding and abetting the enemy, collective punishment of the entire community for Arafat's costly blunder. The remaining Palestinians fled the country.[66] Many of the positions vacated by Palestinians were soon filled by Egyptians and increasingly by qualified Asians, Filipinos, Indians, and Sri Lankans – non-Muslims who were prepared to work under time-bound contracts, but could not claim special consideration as brother Arabs or Muslims. Their employment was regulated by agreements negotiated with their respective governments; recruitment was managed by labor contractors.

Displacement and victimization

Through no fault of their own, members of the thriving Palestinian diaspora in Kuwait were suddenly uprooted, homeless and jobless, illustrating the vulnerability of diasporas that remain aliens in their host country. Displaced for the second time, a few thousand were accepted in Iraq, while the majority found refuge in overcrowded Jordan, the only Arab country that would accept them. This time, they were expelled by fellow Arabs, adding still another painful chapter to the saga of Palestinian displacement and victimization. Those with valid travel documentation from other Arab countries or from Israel were allowed to return to those countries, but as many as 40,000, the majority from Gaza, were stateless, with no place to go. A few were admitted to Canada, the US, Australia, and other countries. Fewer than 40,000, 10 percent of the original diaspora, were eventually allowed to stay or trickle back and gain readmission to Kuwait as resident aliens.

Thus, the thriving Palestinian diaspora in Kuwait was suddenly and violently terminated.

3h. Mexicans in the United States

Descendants of Mexican families that inhabit the six southwestern states of the United States have lived continuously as US citizens since that vast area was annexed to the United States following the Mexican War, 1846–8. Mexicans have been crossing the 2,000-mile contiguous land border with the United States seeking work for well over a century. Most came as sojourners for seasonal employment in agriculture, returning to their homes and families after the harvest. Some, however, chose to remain, settling mainly in the cities of the southwest and in metropolitan Chicago. During the Great Depression of the 1930s, as many as 500,000, including a number of US citizens who looked Mexican, were summarily and brutally deported to Mexico, victims of the prevailing racism.[67] During World War II and until 1964 the congressionally sanctioned "Bracero" program admitted Mexicans for temporary employment as agricultural workers.[68] They were welcomed for their labor, but expected otherwise to remain invisible and cause no trouble. Because of their color, they became victims of discrimination and segregation, practices that diminished but did not disappear after enactment of the Federal civil rights legislation in the mid-1960s.

US supply and demand for low-skilled workers

After 1970 Mexican immigration accelerated, driven by rapid population growth and poor employment prospects in their homeland and attracted by the expanding demand in the US for unskilled, low wage workers in agriculture, construction, manufacturing, landscaping, and domestic service. Since many of these were permanent jobs that paid many times more than they could expect to earn in Mexico with its labor surplus, many chose to remain, settle, and raise families in the US. They followed events in their home country and remitted funds to help hard-pressed families back home. Beginning in the 1990s, they spread out from the southwest to other areas where jobs, some dangerous and dirty, were plentiful, mainly in agriculture, construction, meat packing, poultry processing, hotel and hospital labor, and domestic service.

According to the 2000 census, there were about 10 million legally documented Mexicans and their children in the US, plus another 10 million "undocumented" men and women who had succeeded in crossing the border, evading border guards, entering illegally, finding refuge with relatives and friends in existing Mexican-American communities, and blending into the unskilled labor force.[69] An estimated 500,000 Mexicans enter the United States annually, seeking work.[70] In 2000, the Mexican diaspora comprised 21 percent of the population of California and 23 percent in Texas.

Most Mexican immigrants keep in close touch with their families back home, living what amounts to a transnational existence, intending originally to return home. They take advantage of inexpensive communication and transportation facilities to maintain contact with family members across the border. In the *barrios* (Mexican settlements) in cities in the border states of the southwest, they reproduce the cultural environment they left behind in their former homeland. Mexican entrepreneurs establish businesses that cater to the distinctive culinary, financial, social, lodging, and entertainment needs of the large Mexican diaspora, including Spanish-language radio and television services. The majority soon find it expedient to settle in the US and arrange for their wives, sweethearts, and children to join them.

The 1986 Immigration Reform and Control Act (IRCA) offered to legalize the status of undocumented immigrants who had worked in the US for at least five years. They would first be required to learn English and basic American civics, as stepping stones to naturalization and American citizenship. Around 3 million took advantage of this amnesty to legalize their status, removing the threat of deportation. Their green cards enabled them to move freely about the country in search of employment. IRCA also provided for strengthened border controls and prescribed penalties for employers discovered employing illegal aliens. Neither of these provisions proved effective; few employers were ever sanctioned and the flow of illegal immigrants continued unabated. Many of the 3 million who accepted the amnesty then arranged for their families to join them, swelling the legalized Mexican diaspora. Because Mexican immigrants are a young group, their birth rate considerably exceeds the American norm. Two-thirds of US population growth is now attributed to natural increase.

The politics of Mexican immigration

The politics surrounding the large and conspicuous Mexican diaspora are simple. It created the predictable nativist backlash against what was perceived as a horde of brown-skinned, uneducated foreigners, who speak a strange language and who are accused of "stealing" jobs from American workers, spreading disease, increasing crime, and overwhelming local schools, hospitals, and welfare facilities supported by American taxpayers. Reacting to Federal legislation in 1968 and 1974 that authorized bilingual education, their publics resentful of ubiquitous Spanish-language signs and public notices, 27 states proceeded to enact laws declaring English their state's official language and denying public services to illegal aliens ("law breakers") and their children. Several of these laws were declared unconstitutional by the courts, denying immigrants and their children the equal protection of the law. Nativists with more lurid imaginations visualize Mexican immigrants as the first wave of a campaign to detach the southwest from the United States and reunite it with its former homeland.

Nativist efforts to seal the borders and require employer sanctions have been nullified by three forces. The first and most important of these is pressure from politically influential employer organizations, since many employers welcome and have come to rely on the docile, hard-working, non-union, low-wage Mexican workers and want no interruption in their availability. In fact, many prefer undocumented workers, since the threat of deportation assures their passive acceptance of sub-standard working and living conditions that American workers would not tolerate. Pressure from employers in many communities proved sufficient to overcome resentment by African-Americans and poor Whites at what they considered to be unfair competition for jobs, pressure on low-income housing, and unwelcome incursions into their neighborhoods. The hard economic reality is that several important American industries, including large-scale fruit and vegetable growers, now depend on low-wage Mexican immigrant labor, legal and illegal. Mexicans have become the dominant ethnic group nationally in the construction industry. Owners and managers of such businesses find the occasional raids by immigration officers searching for undocumented workers disruptive to their operations and costly.

The second source of support for undocumented workers and their families has been sympathetic church groups, which regard them as prospective communicants and as fellow humans whose needs supersede the harsh provisions of law. They are joined by labor unions eager to organize, enroll, and represent Mexican workers. Non-government service and advocacy organizations, fostering and protecting human rights, believe that undocumented workers are entitled to their support as victims of racist prejudice, discrimination, and unjust public policy. Together they constitute a formidable coalition.

The third source of support is the voting power of Mexican-American citizens, especially in several states of the southwest. Though Mexican immigrants are slow to naturalize and to participate in politics even when eligible, the sheer number of American citizens among them enables them to influence the results of elections.[71] In California they successfully contributed to defeating the Republican candidate for governor in 1998, penalizing him and his party for sponsoring Resolution 187 in 1994, which would have denied public services, including education, to the children of undocumented (mainly Mexican) parents, followed by Resolution 227 in 1998, which entrenched English as the sole language of instruction and proscribed bilingual instruction in the state's public schools.[72]

Though they have been slow to organize and support advocacy groups, Mexican-American citizens, with the help of sympathetic American foundations, set up such organizations as the Mexican-American Legal Defense and Education

Fund (MALDEF), which works with unions, churches, and human rights agencies to defend the legal rights of Mexican-Americans; and the National Council of La Raza, which mobilizes Mexican-Americans for political action.[73] La Raza encourages Mexican immigrants to naturalize and achieve citizenship so that they can vote. Tough-sounding laws designed to pacify nativist anxieties, to militarize the border, to harass undocumented aliens and their families, and to penalize employers who hire illegals have been underfinanced and indifferently enforced.

An undereducated, unskilled labor diaspora

Mexicans in the US are a labor diaspora, young, poor, undereducated and unskilled.[74] Most are employed in low-wage jobs, as many as 25 percent subsisting in poverty.[75] They have been penalized by the decline in manufacturing industries which offered employment, usually at living wages, to unskilled workers. The few who have succeeded in advancing to the middle class are mostly professionals or owners of small businesses such as shops, restaurants, entertainment and service enterprises catering to Mexican customers. In the *barrios* of the larger Mexican settlements, like Los Angeles, El Paso, and Houston, immigrants can lead lives entirely in a Spanish-language, Mexican cultural ambiance, interacting with mainstream America only in the workplace. They constitute, in effect, a plural society.

Many members of the second, US-born generation, American citizens by birth, fluent in colloquial English, nevertheless do poorly in school, victims of low aspirations and low expectations. Their high school dropout rate, nearly 50 percent, condemns them to the same unskilled, low-wage jobs as their immigrant parents. They encounter a street culture that derides educational effort and superior performance in school as "uncool," fostering an oppositional mentality based on perceived discrimination and affronts to their personal and collective dignity. Among high school graduates, fewer than half obtain jobs that enable them eventually to advance to middle-class status. A mere 7 percent graduate from college and qualify for professional positions.

As in many African-American communities, in some *barrios* Mexican-American dropouts control the streets of low-income neighborhoods, the scene of drug trafficking and petty crime; they shape the youth culture in second-generation circles. They compare their present lot not with Mexicans in the old country, as did their parents, but with mainstream Americans, resulting in a resentful sense of relative deprivation and abused identity. Most of them find employment, however, and the majority attempt a pragmatic accommodation to the demands and opportunities of their American environment.

Cultural assimilation

The Mexican-American diaspora, constantly renewed by streams of fresh recruits, will continue to increase in numbers and in political importance as long as there is demand in the United States for low-wage labor, and wage scales in the US remain substantially higher than those in Mexico. Despite the bi-national environment in which many Mexican immigrants, legal and illegal, continue to function, with frequent return visits to the homeland, easy and cheap communication by telephone and e-mail, continuous remittances of funds to families,[76] as well as dual citizenship and voting rights provided by the Mexican government, the great majority choose to remain and settle in the US. Their children and grandchildren assimilate culturally to the American mainstream, imbibing and contributing to the country's popular culture. Two-thirds of the members of the second generation report that they speak English in their households.[77] Dissatisfied with their limited social mobility and their slow advancement into the middle class, they nevertheless participate increasingly in mainstream economic, educational, and political institutions. As an officially recognized disadvantaged minority, they benefit from affirmative action, especially preferences in university admissions.

A growing number compete for and win elective offices in state and local government. In 1996 Mexican-Americans constituted 20 percent of the Texas House of Representatives and 25 percent of the Texas State Senate. There were 19 Mexican-American members of the US House of Representatives. In 2005 the US Attorney-General, Governor of New Mexico, US Senator from Colorado, and Mayor of Los Angeles were among the more prominent Mexican-Americans in political positions.[78] Mexican-Americans are a growing political force, courted by both political parties. However, they identify overwhelmingly and consistently as Democrats. In 2006, 67.8 percent identified as Democrats, only 15.8 percent as Republican.[79] Yet their turnout has been consistently low. Only 13 percent of eligible Mexican-American voters actually voted in 2006, compared with 39 percent for Anglos and 27 percent for African-Americans.

Mexican-Americans are now the nation's largest ethnic community and their numbers continue to expand, by natural increase and by immigration. Like other ethnic communities, they are by no means a monolithic body. In the border areas, young *Chicanos*, American-born, US citizens, fluent English speakers, look down upon and sometimes clash violently with recent immigrants, taunting them as "wetbacks." Their adaptation to American society and culture varies with their reception in different localities, from urban Los Angeles, Chicago, and New York to small-town Iowa, rural North Carolina, and the eastern shore of Maryland and Delaware; and with the talents and ambitions of individuals.[80]

Though many are thwarted by their limited social mobility, nearly all succeed in finding employment, while the second and third generations acculturate to the mainstream popular culture and participate in the American way of life. A number enlist in the military and emerge with employable skills, opportunity for subsidized higher education and home ownership, and pride in their American citizenship.[81] A third intermarry, thus assimilating into the American mainstream. There are periodic violent, even lethal, clashes in the Los Angeles area, known as the gang capital of the world. African-American youth gangs complain that the more numerous Mexicans are invading their neighborhoods and challenging control of their turf, including the lucrative drug trade. Between January and June 2007, there were 102 gang-related homicides in the Los Angeles area.[82]

In many urban areas where Mexicans and African-Americans coexist, the latter claim that the more numerous Mexican immigrants encroach on their housing, speak only Spanish, steal their jobs, and presume to challenge the political power that African-Americans have only recently wrested from an entrenched White establishment. There, African-Americans fight to hold on to their hard-won political spoils. African-Americans and Mexicans have developed unflattering images of each other. To Mexican-Americans, Blacks are lazy and prefer to live on government handouts. To African-Americans, Mexicans are foreigners, willing to work for slave wages and refusing to learn to speak American.

Nevertheless, Mexican-Americans join African-Americans in identifying politically with the Democratic Party, which supports and sponsors government services for low-income individuals, while its Republican opponents proclaim their hostility to immigrants. Like African-Americans, Mexican-Americans continue to complain of racist profiling and harassment by the police.[83] During the 2007–8 Democratic Party's presidential preference campaign, a great majority of African-Americans supported Barack Obama, who happens to be Black, while Mexicans and other Hispanics refused to support a Black candidate and overwhelmingly favored his principal opponent, Hillary Clinton. In the presidential election, however, Mexican-Americans voted overwhelmingly for Obama, helping him to win the Southwestern states of Nevada, New Mexico, and Colorado.

In July 2007, the newly elected Democratic majority in Congress supported an initiative by President George W. Bush that would have provided an opportunity for undocumented residents, mostly Mexicans, who had lived and worked in the United States continuously for five years or more to qualify as legally resident aliens with the possibility of earning citizenship. It was bitterly obstructed and eventually defeated by a determined Republican minority responding to widespread opposition among their nativist constituents to "amnesty" for law-breakers. In 2006 the previous Republican-dominated Congress had authorized a large increase in the number of border patrol officers and the construction of a 700-mile wall at a section of the border most frequently penetrated by Mexican emigrants. Beneath the surface, the intensity of this opposition could be interpreted as the expression of lingering xenophobia and racism.[84]

The American opportunity structure continues to accept, if it does not fully welcome, legal immigrants of all ethnic backgrounds, including Mexicans, if they support themselves, obey the law, learn English, and demonstrate interest in qualifying for citizenship – in becoming American. Members of the Mexican diaspora who enter the country legally have, for the most part, agreed to become American. Except for a small group of intellectuals, there has been no pressure on the part of Mexican immigrants or their American-born children to reject American society or to demand recognition as a culturally or politically separate community. Despite their frustrations, there have been no violent mass protests similar to those of African-Americans in the 1960s or the recent demonstrations by north African youths in France.

The problem of the undocumented

Americans are divided, however, on policies toward the millions of undocumented immigrants, the majority of whom are Mexicans. These undocumented immigrants make their perilous way to the United States, seeking and usually finding work. Americans agree that immigration laws should be more strictly enforced and borders made more secure. But what should be done with the millions of undocumented immigrants, the majority Mexican, already living and working in the country, far too many to consider deporting? What, for example, of illegal nursing mothers whose US-born children are American citizens; should they be deported and separated from their children? What would be the economic effects of suddenly depriving employers of their indispensable services? Until their status has been decided, millions of undocumented Mexican immigrants continue to exist in the United States in a legal no man's land, needed for their labor, but vulnerable to apprehension and summary deportation. Most likely a formula can be found that avoids "amnesty," but provides legal status and a path to citizenship for the millions of undocumented Mexican-Americans who have lived and worked continuously in the United States for several years. They would then be permitted to join the ranks of Mexican-Americans who, with each successive generation in the country, intensify their acculturation to the English language and mainstream lifestyle, and integrate more deeply into mainstream society. Like other Americanizing communities, they leave their distinctive mark on mainstream culture and become a force in national, state, and local politics.

During the 1990s the United States experienced the largest wave of immigrants in its history, at least a third of whom originated in Mexico. Despite continuing nativist suspicion, the US remains the classic immigrant society, tolerating diversity, as long as immigrants and their American-born offspring are prepared to accommodate to American institutions and the American way of life. This permits Mexican immigrants to establish themselves as useful participants in the US economy and as candidates for citizenship.[85] As Christians, Mexican-Americans are welcome in America's dominant Catholic and Protestant churches. The upward mobility of Mexican-Americans is constrained partly by lingering but diminishing racial prejudice, but mainly by low educational achievement, a common handicap for labor diasporas. Mexican-Americans are pressured to learn and use English, but not to "whiten" their appearance. While they are free to remain in their *barrios* in low-wage employment, the inclusive opportunity structure in the United States is open to them as individuals in the educational, political, military, and economic institutions of American society, as long as they are prepared to participate and compete.

The boundary between the Mexican diaspora and mainstream America is fluid. Second and subsequent generations of the Mexican diaspora can and do pass through this boundary, leaving the diaspora communities behind. Nevertheless, in their recently published study of several generations of Mexican-Americans in Los Angeles, California and San Antonio, Texas, Telles and Ortiz found rapid acculturation to the English language combined with widespread persistence of ethnic identity. "Among fourth generation Mexican-Americans, most live in majority Hispanic neighborhoods . . . most frequently think of themselves as Mexican . . . although intermarriage with other groups tends to grow with each generation . . . by the fourth generation nearly two thirds are still married to other Hispanics . . . although they may have lost some ethnic cultural attributes like language, most . . . experience a world largely shaped by their race and ethnicity." Poor educational performance retards their occupational and social mobility and delays their integration into the American mainstream.[86]

Few economically or professionally successful Mexican-Americans choose to remain in the *barrios*.[87] What they retain of their ethnic identity and culture are dual citizenship, a sense of obligation to assist family members in their former homeland, and nostalgic memories that diminish with passing generations as more and more descendants of Mexican immigrants assimilate culturally and socially into the American mainstream.[88] The Mexican diaspora will, however, be sustained as long as there are fresh arrivals who need the security, services, and opportunities afforded by its institutions until they or their children develop the ability to cope with America on their own.

4
Problems and processes of adaptation

Adaptation to their new environment: this is the principal challenge to all diaspora communities. *Diaspora inclinations* and *local opportunity structures*: these are the critical interacting factors that condition the adaptation of diaspora communities to their host countries.

A separate community?

If a diaspora's elites and opinion leaders are determined to maintain their inherited culture and separate collective identity; and if they are able to discipline their members and control their early socialization; and especially if their collective identity is fortified by distinctive religious convictions and sanctions, then they may succeed in their intention to remain a separate community in their new homeland. Diasporas that regard their culture as superior to the culture and lifestyles that they encounter in their host country and, in addition, gain a unique set of niches in the local economy, may prefer to remain separate.

The determination to remain separate is strengthened when the local opportunity structure is revealed as hostile, when it excludes or discriminates against them, and when it blocks or penalizes their access to education, employment, business opportunities, and political participation. When they encounter such blockages, members of diasporas are deprived of incentives to break away from the shelter of their community. As this occurs, the diaspora may remain a separate community, cultivate its separate culture and institutions, and manage its own affairs indefinitely. Turks in Germany, north Africans in France, Indians in east Africa, and Amish in Canada are examples of diaspora communities that either prefer to remain separate or encounter an unwelcoming opportunity structure.

An unwelcoming opportunity structure may be encountered either by blockages of access to educational, economic, and political participation, or by demonstrations of contempt or disrespect for the culture of an immigrant community and for its members. In the latter case, the dominant establishment equates racial and cultural difference with inferiority. What stigmatizes the group stigmatizes its individual members as well and leaves a residue of bitterness. This may be underscored by the perception that immigrants are competing unfairly with native sons for scarce housing and jobs, and with local businesses by employing sharp or unscrupulous tactics. Most Europeans regard the Muslim culture of their Turkish, north African and south Asian diasporas as inferior to their own, and thus not entitled to respect. They believe it to be the duty of immigrants as newcomers to make an honest effort to adopt the language and lifestyle of the national mainstream, and to qualify for citizenship on terms set by mainstream authority. Perceived failure of the second, locally born generation to make that effort is interpreted as hostility, justifying continued suspicion and marginalization both by government and by mainstream society. Those who refuse to conform, so the argument runs, should go back where they came from.

Spokespersons for diaspora communities that prefer to remain separate assert culture maintenance as a human right that all governments are required to respect.[1] The right to remain separate is reinforced when local society demonstrates little inclination to accord their culture and their persons the dignity and respect to which they believe they are entitled. The unwillingness of French society and government to respect the religious requirements of observant north African Muslims by barring headscarves from public schools, foot-dragging by the European Union on Turkey's long-standing application for admission, and the resistance of German communities to the construction of mosques send messages to Turkish immigrants and their locally born children that Europeans disrespect them and their culture and refuse to accept them as equals. Why, then, should they pursue membership in the French or German political community, only to be treated as second class?

When elites attempt to commit their diaspora community to a separate existence, but the local opportunity structure permits, even encourages, access to and participation in mainstream institutions, then a struggle takes place within the community. How shall they adapt to the local society? We have noted in chapter 2 that diaspora communities are never monolithic. Elites may attempt to strengthen the solidarity of the community and to maintain its integrity, making as few concessions as possible to the local culture and society. However, some members on the margins respond to the opportunities offered by mainstream institutions and find its lifestyles appealing. They break away from the discipline of the diaspora community, participate in mainstream institutions, and adopt its lifestyles. To limit defections, the diaspora leadership both tightens community discipline and tolerates minor changes in lifestyles intended to lessen the appeal of the mainstream to younger members. Young Hasidim in the United States are permitted to play baseball and basketball, but are forbidden to adopt mainstream dress.

Two stages of adaptation

There are two dimensions and two stages of adaptation by members of diaspora communities to host societies. The first is *acculturation*: acceptance and adoption of basic elements of the local culture, its language and lifestyle, its methods of working and popular entertainment, its dress codes and cuisine. Even among diasporas that rate their inherited culture above and superior to the local culture, their survival and ability to function in their host environment require at least minimal acculturation – learning, for example to communicate in an understandable version of the local language. The second, locally born, locally reared generation is likely to proceed many steps farther in the direction of acculturation, acquiring linguistic fluency and absorbing many features of the local culture and its lifestyles.

The second dimension of adaptation is participation in the networks of mainstream institutions – educational, economic, religious, and political – leading eventually to *social assimilation*, absorption into the local mainstream, and acceptance of citizenship, culminating often in intermarriage. At any point in time, members of diasporas may retard, or they may accelerate, their pace of social assimilation, depending on the prevailing incentives, their propensity to adapt to the mainstream, and the willingness of the mainstream to accept them into its ranks. It is at this stage that individuals evolve hybrid identities, membership and participation in both the diaspora and the host society culture and society. They use the one or the other as the situation dictates: for example, the diaspora language at home, and the language of the host society at school and work.

These two dimensions of adaptation are both analytically and empirically distinct. Acculturation may be nearly complete, while social assimilation is blocked – the experience of Afro-Brazilians. The grandparents of the 2.7 million-strong Turkish diaspora in Germany were recruited to overcome a severe post-World War II labor shortage. Now in its third generation, having acculturated to the mainstream language, dress code, and employment methods, Turkish-Germans nevertheless limit their participation in mainstream German institutions. They cling to their Islamic faith. Barely a third of eligible Turkish-Germans have accepted German citizenship.

Their dropout rate from high schools is three times the German average. While continuing to live and work in Germany, paying its taxes and enjoying its welfare benefits, but sensing the ethnocentric hostility of rank-and-file Germans, the majority choose to remain resident aliens in a separate, parallel diaspora community. They follow political developments in Turkey often with greater interest than events in their adopted country.[2]

Turkish-German spokesmen assert that until the recent liberalization, requirements for naturalization were so daunting that many Turkish-Germans were discouraged from even trying. That Germany does not permit dual citizenship constitutes an additional disincentive. There is the further feeling that Germany's government and society show little respect for their culture or religion. Unlike Catholicism, Protestantism and Judaism, Islam in Germany is not an officially recognized religion.[3] The construction of Islamic houses of worship all too often evokes fierce resistance and public controversy that would be unthinkable for Christian churches or Jewish synagogues. Several *Land* (state) governments refuse to allow Turkish students or teachers to wear headscarves in public schools, despite a ruling by the federal Constitutional Court that neither the Federal Parliament nor state governments can limit the free expression of religious convictions. Until more respect is shown for Turkish culture and religion, could they expect to be treated as equal? Would they be welcome as members of Germany's political community even if they were to accept German citizenship? Or would they be relegated to second-class membership?

Could Germany's governments and publics be induced to show greater respect for Turkish culture and religion? If so, would Turkish-Germans be more inclined to embrace German culture, accept German citizenship, and participate in the institutions of German society? Would Germans, in turn, agree to permit dual citizenship and treat Turkish compatriots as equals? Would the Turkish-German community find it possible to evolve a European version of Islam? These are suggestive of the mutual accommodation that will be required by both sides if Muslim diasporas in Germany and elsewhere in Europe, the majority born and reared in Europe, are to identify as European and integrate into European societies. The alternative prospect is large permanent resident communities of disaffected aliens, needed for their labor and too numerous to deport, confronting European nations with chronic threats to their security and stability.

Anti-Muslim hysteria in Europe

The Muslim presence in Europe has generated a wave of hysteria among some pundits and their readers in Europe and America. They regard the Muslim diaspora, some of whose fanatics have plotted, threatened, and committed terrorist acts against civilian targets, as "Islamofascists," forerunners of a vast conspiracy to Islamize Europe. They are believed to have no interest in integrating into Europe's secular, democratic societies. Continuing immigration, much of it illegal, combined with very high birth rates and the failure of the current European generation to reproduce its numbers, guarantees, they argue, that within several decades the exploding Muslim population growth will enable their diasporas peacefully, without firing a shot, to gain control of Europe and annex it to the nation of Islam.[4] Having used Europe's democratic institutions to win control of Europe's governments, they would then proceed to destroy these institutions and establish Islamic theocracies in their stead. Germans, French, Dutch, English would be pressured to convert to Islam or be reduced to tolerated minorities in their own countries.

This Islamophobic scenario is not shared by most Europeans. In response to an August 2007 survey, less than two years after the north African riots of October 2005, only 20 percent of French respondents agreed that the "presence of Muslims in your country poses a threat to national security;" 68 percent disagreed, while 12 percent were not sure.[5] No more than 30 percent of respondents in the major countries of western Europe, all of which have experienced terrorist acts committed by Muslims, agreed with this proposition. The exception was Britain. There, 38 percent saw Muslims as a threat to national security, 45 percent disagreeing. This poll demonstrates that, though a significant minority of Europeans are fearful and distrustful of Islamic diasporas in their country, substantial majorities do not harbor these fears.

When diasporas face exclusion, they perforce remain separate societies. Under more favorable conditions they weigh competing pressures to join the mainstream, to maintain a separate collective identity and a distinctive community, or to adopt an intermediate position that enables them to enjoy the best of both worlds. Many Chinese-Canadians participate actively in mainstream political and economic institutions, while taking advantage of Canada's multicultural program to recreate a Chinese-language cultural presence in their new surroundings.

Women tend to exert a conservative influence for maintaining diaspora cultures and slowing the pace of integration. In most societies, women, less well educated than their menfolk, are confined to household and domestic activities. They have fewer opportunities and fewer incentives to adopt the language and lifestyles of their host societies. They are thus more inclined than men to preserve the familiar language, customs, and lifestyles that they brought with them from the old country. This cultural conservatism among women applies particularly to the immigrant cohort and declines with subsequent, locally born generations as young women, through schooling and access to mass media, acculturate to the mainstream language, economic roles, and lifestyles – including the equality of status – enjoyed by European women.

Grievances and their mitigation

Laws mandating acceptance of ethnic diversity and criminalizing discrimination can embolden diaspora members to assert their right to equal treatment. Laws and public policies can begin to alter deep-seated convictions and behavior, but only if accompanied by persistent advocacy and strict enforcement. In the absence of vigorous enforcement against reluctant landlords and employers, and in the face of deep-seated prejudice and continuing hostility in mainstream circles, such well-intentioned legal initiatives, as in Brazil, can prove to be little more than aspirations for an indefinite future. The benefits to diasporas are symbolic and, probably, deferred.

Leading personalities in diaspora communities sometimes find it necessary to demand the mitigation of grievances or to request favors for members of the community that only those in positions of authority can grant. To achieve the necessary access, they may work through formal channels, such as government bureaucracies, elected officials, mass media, or the courts. If, for example, they are protesting job discrimination in the recruitment of police cadets, they might first try the police department's official channels; failing that, elected representatives or the courts, asserting violations of non-discrimination statutes by the police department. They may find, however, that for some matters, informal channels provide better access. Political brokers or fixers may prove more effective than their formal counterparts in reaching those who control resources and implement policies. Leaders of religious associations, labor unions, peasant associations, and business groups may perform this function.[6]

In some instances, a member of the political establishment takes the diaspora community under his or her wing in a patron–client relationship, funneling the diaspora's demands to political decision-makers or to private enterprises, in return for discrete financial payments or for services, such as assistance and support during election campaigns. Requests for favors may involve individual cases, such as springing a petty law-breaker from prison, or matters that affect large numbers, such as a flood control project for a large neighborhood.

Because of factions within diasporas, there may be more than one group seeking favorable access to decision-makers. In Malaysia, members of the Chinese business community may deal with the Malay-dominated government through the Malayan Chinese Association (MCA), the political vehicle of the Chinese business community. As the junior partner in the ruling coalition, the MCA is able to deliver campaign funds and an important bloc of Chinese votes at election time. Members of the Chinese opposition faction are at a distinct disadvantage. They can attempt to reach government through its bureaucratic agencies or their elected representatives on the opposition benches of Parliament; or, more effectively, through informal channels by individual brokers or professional associations. The fact that the MCA has privileged access to government decision-makers guarantees it a hearing, but not necessarily satisfaction. After many years of petitions and pressure, it was successful in gaining approval for a private university serving mostly Chinese youth, but as yet it has been unsuccessful in urging the ending of preferences for Malays in the awarding of government contracts or in admissions to the government's network of universities.

Half-way adjustments and dual identities

Individuals acculturate and participate in mainstream institutions at different rates, evolving a number of half-way adjustments between assimilation and complete separation. They may embrace mainstream identity and lifestyles, participate in mainstream institutions and take up residence in mainstream neighborhoods, yet continue for some purposes to associate and identify with diaspora institutions and culture. This is true in Canada, where the government sponsors and finances a version of multiculturalism. The large Ukrainian community centered in Manitoba has adopted Canadian mainstream English-speaking culture and lifestyles, while attempting to preserve elements of its inherited culture and retain the participation of its third-generation offspring. Defending elderly compatriots accused – falsely, they believe – of having committed anti-Semitic atrocities during World War II mobilized the Ukrainian diaspora and reinforced its solidarity, given its determination to vindicate the honor of its community and their nation. (This contrasts with the fate of the large German-Canadian diaspora in southwestern Ontario centered in Kitchener, formerly Berlin. The shock of World War I forced them to resist the charge of dual loyalty by emphasizing their Canadian patriotism, soft-pedaling their inherited culture, and blending fully into the Anglo-Canadian mainstream.)

In the process of collective adaptation, individuals may arrive at distinctive adjustments that can endure for long periods of time. Members of the immigrant generation, having acculturated to the mainstream language, enjoy elements of the mainstream culture – its athletic events, popular music, and entertainment – yet their economic efforts may be confined to niche enterprises operated by compatriots within their ethnic cocoon. Members of the second generation, locally educated, more confident of their capabilities, are more inclined to take their chances in mainstream institutions when such opportunities become available. If successful, they may move out of diaspora neighborhoods, adopt mainstream lifestyles, possibly intermarry. Nevertheless, because of nostalgia, respect for elderly parents, or a sense of obligation, individuals may maintain links with diaspora institutions, even after they have abandoned diaspora culture and its way of life. They contrive to participate fully in mainstream culture and society, but without abandoning their ethnic heritage and links with the institutions of the diaspora. Maintaining, in effect, a dual, split, or hybrid identity, they draw on whichever one seems appropriate to the circumstances. Working in a mainstream enterprise, they function as mainstream individuals. In their parents' home and neighborhood, they revert to their ethnic identity. With each successive generation, however, this combination becomes less feasible, as the mainstream identity eclipses the fading influence of their diaspora heritage.

Diaspora communities that adhere to a distinctive religious tradition are especially prone to adopt a dual or hybrid identity. Their members adopt a mainstream political identity and participate actively in its institutions, while preserving an attachment to their inherited religious traditions and practices. Greek-Americans, Jewish-Americans, and Indian-Australians represent examples of this dual identity, connected politically and economically to the national mainstream, while maintaining their separate religious affiliation. France's political elites are hopeful that their north African community will eventually adopt this strategy, following the lead of that nation's Jewish community. They would identify politically as French, participate in mainstream educational and economic institutions, and adopt mainstream French lifestyles, while continuing to adhere to, identify with, and practice a European version of their religious tradition. France's Muslim elites would reform their religious practices to align them with the requirements of a democratic, secular society. This hopeful development cannot, however, be realized until France's government and society abandon their discriminatory attitudes and practices, and begin to accept French-born members of that diaspora as fellow citizens, entitled to equal, respectful treatment: in short, until the opportunity structure encountered by the Maghrebi diaspora affords it realizable incentives to identify with and participate in mainstream French institutions.

France's predicament with its Muslim diaspora is replicated throughout contemporary Europe. Turks in Germany, Pakistanis in Britain, and Moroccans in Spain all face similar problems of adjustment to their host country. Would the incentives of an open opportunity structure enable them to adopt mainstream culture, participate in mainstream institutions, and assume a mainstream European identity, while continuing to adhere to their separate religious faith?

Such an adjustment would require mutual accommodation. Europeans would need to be willing to accept an unfamiliar diversity, a racially distinct Muslim religious presence in their midst, endowed with equality of rights and status for members of that visible minority. Are the French, German, Spaniards, Dutch willing to expand the definition of their national community to include, as equals, the racially and culturally diverse minorities that have been admitted to their countries for economic reasons? And are Muslim diasporas, in turn, prepared to evolve a reformed version of Islam that is compatible with European civilization, that can coexist comfortably with European conceptions of human rights and democracy, including equality for women and separation of church and state? And accept the duties and responsibilities of citizenship, cultivating a sense of belonging to their adopted countries?

Factions and their uses

The pace of adaptation is complicated by the reality of factions. As political institutions, diaspora communities are hosts to cleavages that reflect, and often represent, competing ideologies, class interests, regional origins, kinship loyalties, and personal ambitions. In the course of adaptation, a diaspora may split into factions. "Modernists" advocate acculturation to the mainstream and acceptance, where possible, of citizenship in their host country, while sustaining their affiliation with the diaspora and attachment to its culture. They construct, in effect, dual or hybrid identities. Failure to adapt, they insist, risks the loss of younger members and condemns them to backwardness and eventual irrelevance. "Traditionalists" demand strict adherence to their inherited culture and a minimum of necessary concessions to local institutions and lifestyles, mainly to economic activities required for survival. Failure to maintain their ancestral traditions and way of life would, they argue, result inevitably in the gradual disintegration of their community. In larger diaspora, such as Jewish-Americans and Chinese-Canadians, several intermediate factions may emerge, each arguing that its particular pattern of adjustment is the preferable course of action for the well-being of its members and the maintenance of their community.[7] Others choose to join the mainstream and abandon their community altogether.

Among those who have chosen integration, reactive responses may be observed among members of the third and successor generations. Having successfully acculturated to the mainstream and participated fully in mainstream institutions, some individuals begin to sense an emptiness in their identity that precipitates a search for "roots." In most cases what they discover may amount to little more than a curiosity, as mainstream culture and lifestyles consume their energies and command their identities. Yet, some quests for roots involve a search for authenticity, as individuals grope for a pseudo-identity, a romantic association with the old country and the culture and lifestyle that their grandparents had left behind. Thus, some apparently assimilated Jews rediscover and embrace religious orthodoxy and its separate disciplines and lifestyles, turning their backs on the integrationist strategy pursued by their modernist parents. In so doing, they may forgo some mainstream opportunities – the price they are willing to pay to recover a lost authentic identity.

Bottom-line issues

Despite the conflicts that rage among them, as they contend for control of the diaspora's resources and the right to speak for the diaspora in its relations with outsiders, there are bottom-line issues on which diasporas stand united. The Armenian diaspora is united in its insistence that the government of Turkey acknowledge and apologize for the genocide of 1915–16, but it is split on tactics to pursue in confronting the Turkish state, successor to the Ottoman Empire. A minority has favored direct action, including assassination of Turkish officials, while the majority prefers to rely on public relations and diplomatic pressure. While the Jewish diaspora is split among several religious factions, and Zionists have been divided among contending labor, religious, revisionist, and "general" camps, since Israel's independence in 1948 they have been united in their bottom-line commitment to the country's security, while favoring different factions and competing policies within Israel's polity.

Recognizing the reality of internal divisions, we neverthe-less identify and highlight what we observe to be the *central tendency* within each diaspora community. This central tendency reflects the preferences and the behavior of the diaspora's opinion leaders and the majority of its members. In every diaspora, however, there are likely to be outliers, individuals and groups that depart from the central tendency of their community. There are, for example, Malaysian-Chinese who have converted to Islam, and north Africans in France who have achieved economic success in business or have become active in mainstream political parties. The examples of such outliers do not undermine the central tendency of their community: Malaysian-Chinese expect to remain a separate community, while north Africans in France remain a disaffected, low-income, economically deprived labor diaspora.

Changes over time

Adaptation strategies can change over time in response to changing circumstances. The adaptation of diasporas is influenced both by their internal dynamics and by changes in their external environment. One of the most significant internal factors is intergenerational change, especially differences between the first, migrating generation, and their locally born, second-generation offspring. The second, locally born, locally educated generation, fluent in the local language, acquainted with mainstream ways of working and popular culture, is likely to enjoy different capabilities and different aspirations than their immigrant parents. The reference group that they aspire to emulate is successful members of mainstream society, not like their parents, respected individuals in their country of origin. With each successive generation they become more indigenized, more remote from the immigrant experience. The local opportunity structure may encourage, or it may constrain, their impulses to participate in mainstream institutions. Combined with their inclination to participate or alternatively to remain separate, the opportunity structure determines their pattern of adaptation to their host society.

The Polish diaspora encountered a welcoming environment in France and has integrated successfully into the French mainstream. Most north Africans, on the other hand, sensing hostility among their hosts, encountering police harassment and dead-end career prospects, have spurned French citizenship. If the second and successive generations encounter an encouraging environment, plus an inclination to take advantage of opportunities to participate in mainstream institutions, social assimilation is likely to follow. Unless renewed by fresh flows of recruits, such diasporas may eventually disappear from history, like the Swedish and Dutch diasporas in the United States. Experience with discrimination and exclusion is certain to solidify a sense of grievance and victimization within a diaspora, magnify its differences from the mainstream, and justify its continuity as a separate community with its own culture and institutions.

The external environment encountered by a diaspora may change, prompting changes in its adaptation strategy. By law and by practice, the United States excluded Asians from entering the country and marginalized those whose ancestors had previously been admitted. The small Chinese diaspora was relegated to laundry and restaurant enterprises that emphasized their separate identity. Japanese, including US citizens, were herded into concentration camps as enemy aliens during the Pacific War. As a result of the successful civil rights revolution by African-Americans, racial discrimination became morally and politically offensive.

Following the civil rights reforms in 1965, immigration reform legislation eliminated discrimination by race and ethnicity. Korean, Chinese, and other Asians entered the US in large numbers. As entrepreneurial diasporas, they acculturated rapidly to the American mainstream and participated actively in mainstream institutions. More than 50 percent of Japanese-Americans now marry outside their ethnic ranks; they and their offspring join the mainstream. In their case, radical changes in the opportunity structure prompted radical changes in their adaptation strategies.[8]

Classic middleman minorities, Indians in east Africa, Chinese in southeast Asia, became economically dominant diasporas, once the former European colonists had departed. Considering their culture superior to those they encountered in the indigenous society, they demonstrated no inclination to acculturate or to integrate into the local mainstream. Invariably they became unpopular, economically affluent but politically weak. Resented because of their unwillingness to integrate into local society, they served as convenient scapegoats, vulnerable targets of ambitious native intellectuals and politicians. Their wealth was believed to have been gained by sharp business practices and by exploiting indigenous people. The hostility generated by their presence focused on their supposed ill-gotten wealth and on the impression that they disrespect their host society.

Victimization

Collective memory of victimization can mobilize and sustain the solidarity of diaspora communities and retard their absorption into the mainstream. The belief, updated in the process of socialization, that their people have sustained atrocities in the past, and even threats to their very existence, such as the Armenian genocide, the Jewish Holocaust, and the Ukrainian famine reinforce their current solidarity. Historical memory of victimization, even in the distant past, evokes sentiments of obligation among current descendants to honor the memory of its victims and ensure that such atrocities are not repeated, to defend their people against future attacks, and to insist that its perpetrators and their descendants at least acknowledge, accept collective responsibility, make amends, and apologize for the crimes committed by their forebears. The psalmist enjoined his fellow Hebrew victims, in their Babylonian exile, not to forget Jerusalem, but to continue to honor and cherish it "above their chief joy," and to maintain their faith and solidarity until the good Lord should see fit to enable them to return.[9] Two millennia later, the grandchildren of Palestinians displaced from their homes in Palestine, believing themselves to be victims of a great injustice, are admonished in their exile to sustain their faith that one day their disaster will be avenged and they will be allowed to reclaim their grandparents' homes.

When combined in the same diaspora community with a distinctive religious heritage, as among Jews and Armenians, the historical memory of victimization creates strong pressures for ethnic maintenance.

Visible diasporas

"Visible" diasporas, those that differ racially from the dominant majority, are likely to encounter special difficulties in gaining acceptance and capitalizing on opportunities available in the host society. Even after they have successfully acculturated, discrimination and marginalization may persist after such practices have been outlawed by governments. The obstacles that continue to be faced by Afro-Brazilians after several centuries, and more recently in Europe by dark-skinned natives of Africa and the Middle East, attest to the racist realities that continue to confront "visible" immigrants. Laws proscribing racial discrimination provide the *formal* scaffolding for the toleration and eventual acceptance of a racially diverse society. Yet *informally*, among police, landlords, employers, and voters, racial discrimination may persist. Asian and Hispanic immigrants in the United States and Canada are more acceptable in today's more liberal environment than in the past, but their integration remains slower and encounters more obstacles than, for example, European immigrants, especially those from northern and western Europe.

Cultural accommodation

As individuals adjust to mainstream culture, so these cultures adjust to their diasporas. Diasporas that integrate into the mainstream leave their mark on mainstream cultures. As markers of their acceptance, mainstream culture incorporates elements, however superficial, from their diasporas. *Bagels*, *pizza*, and *tacos* have been incorporated into mainstream American cuisine; *chutzpah*, *gourmet*, and *numero uno* into mainstream parlance. Language, cuisine, music, and clothing styles are manifestations of popular culture that facilitate the adjustment of the mainstream to its diaspora communities and signal its willingness to accept members of these diasporas. When the mainstream rejects and marginalizes a diaspora, cultural exchange tends to be limited to the diaspora learning sufficient language for economic survival. Even under these conditions, however, cultural exchange may be possible. The Brazilian mainstream, which continues to marginalize its large, longstanding Afro-Brazilian diaspora, has borrowed heavily from its cuisine, music, drama, and speech patterns, and admires and rewards the prowess of gifted Afro-Brazilian athletes. While mainstream France holds its north African diaspora at arm's length, it has become chic among left-leaning youth to patronize cafés featuring north African music, cuisine, and entertainment.

Diaspora organizations

Diasporas generate organizations that facilitate their adaptation to their new environment, serving both the expressive and instrumental needs of their members. *Expressive* organizations are oriented to the maintenance and further development of the diaspora's ethnic culture in their new environment. Theatre, music, art, literature, museums, and athletics are activities facilitated by expressive organizations and their networks. Under its multicultural programs, the government of Canada subsidizes the cultural institutions of its diaspora communities and facilitates their activities. A Yiddish Art Theatre flourished in New York during the decades when the large Jewish immigration was adapting to the American environment. Several writers and performers – Paul Muni, for example, who later starred in Broadway and Hollywood – were trained and had their start in this institution.[10]

Instrumental organizations strive to meet the community's practical needs for religious, economic, social, and educational adjustments to the circumstances they encounter in the diaspora. These range from deposit and loan clubs and burial societies to fraternal associations and classes in the diaspora tongue and in the mainstream language. Diaspora organizations provide opportunities for members to interact with one another in meaningful roles, for some to compete for offices and exercise leadership skills, and to represent their community in dealings with host society officialdom and local publics. They strengthen group solidarity and self-esteem, while helping members accommodate to the opportunities and limitations of the host society. These *voluntary organizations* are in addition to the numerous *for-profit* commercial firms that spring up in diaspora communities, such as restaurants and cafés, grocery stores, travel, insurance, real estate, and insurance agencies. Some such organizations, in time, reach out beyond the diaspora. The Bank of Italy in America, originally serving the Italian diaspora in California, has since expanded into the Bank of America, one of the largest and most powerful financial institutions in the United States.[11]

A distinctively American innovation is the diaspora "defense" organization, a professionally staffed agency dedicated to countering false rumors, discriminatory legislation, or other governmentally or community-inspired measures deemed hostile or defamatory to its ethnic sponsors and the community it represents. Publicity, educational materials, legislative lobbying, and judicial intervention are the main activities of such organizations. The Anti-Defamation League of B'nai B'rith (ADL) and the Mexican-American Legal Defense and Education Fund (MALDEF) are prominent examples of diaspora-sponsored defense organizations that are active on the American scene.[12]

Adaptation to their new, strange environment is the principal challenge facing diaspora communities and their individual members. Once the pioneers have laid the ground-work for the community, made the initial adjustment, and established its main institutions, those that follow have an easier time of it. They need only to fit in until they feel ready to impress their own preferences on the community, strengthening existing organizations or establishing new ones that complement or compete with their predecessors.

This chapter has explored the twin, interacting dimensions of diaspora experiences with adaptation. The first is the *inclination of diaspora communities to integrate* into the local mainstream, or to maintain a separate collective identity. Diaspora communities are likely to opt for integration unless they 1) encounter an unwelcoming opportunity structure, or 2) are bound together by the obligations of a distinctive religious tradition. As they acculturate to the mainstream and participate in its institutions, they may still attempt to retain elements of their inherited culture.

The second is the *opportunity structure* that greets them. Where it encourages and facilitates integration, members of the diaspora are likely to respond favorably. But where the mainstream government and society erect barriers of discrimination, disrespect, and exclusion, the diaspora will turn inward and drift toward separation. A mainstream culture that is aggressively ethnocentric will be hostile to foreigners in its midst, even when they are essential to the operation of its economy; it will confront them with an unwelcoming opportunity structure, then deplore the presence of a disaffected alien community.

Members of a diaspora may make their individual adjustments to their host country outside the central tendency of their community. They may construct split or hybrid identities that enable them to function in both diaspora and mainstream institutions. Or they may abandon the diaspora entirely.

5
Diasporas and international relations

Non-state actors have in recent years encroached on traditional principles of international relations and international law.[1] These principles had limited the international order and actors in the international arena to territorially bounded states, each pursuing its own security and economic interests. States were deemed to be sovereign over their territory and its inhabitants, so that no outsider could legitimately interfere in their internal affairs, except where authorized by treaty.[2] Ideally, each state served as the homeland of a single nation. Members of ethnic minorities and outsiders allowed into the country as permanent residents were expected to blend into the mainstream.

A challenge to this order first originated from the activities of transnational corporations and financial institutions that operate globally, control substantial resources, and can often dictate terms and conditions for trading and investing within states in which they intend to do business. Radio, television, and the internet have eroded the sovereignty of states over information available to their subjects. In the wake of economic and informational globalization, a large number of non-government, not-for-profit organizations (NGOs) has emerged, each promoting and defending its charitable, service, or advocacy concerns across national borders.

For example, Doctors Without Borders, founded by a group of French medical specialists, raises funds and recruits personnel from sympathizers in several industrialized countries and provides medical and health services in low-income countries, including some in countries experiencing insurrections and civil wars.[3] Other NGOs are committed to extending and protecting human rights (for example, Amnesty International), promoting environmental protection (for example, Greenpeace), providing developmental assistance to low-income communities (for example, Oxfam), or spreading their religious faith (for example, Catholic Relief Services), combined in some cases with charitable and developmental activities.

NGOs typically raise funds from sympathizers in wealthier countries and negotiate agreements with governments in host countries that allow them to operate within their borders. A unique variety of NGOs is the diaspora community. I have identified nine kinds of activity by which diasporas impinge on international relations.

1. *Members of many diaspora communities, especially their immigrant generation, maintain a transnational existence.* Physically and occupationally in their host country, they remain socially and culturally in the homeland that they have left behind. As many as a third eventually return to their homeland after an extended stay in their host country. They listen to radio broadcasts from their homeland, follow newspapers and journals on the internet, remain in close touch with relatives and friends, visit their homeland frequently, remit funds to their families, follow political and athletic events, contribute funds to their favorite political parties and candidates, and, where possible, vote in national and local elections. A number of Russian immigrants in Israel, having been awarded Israeli citizenship on arrival, nevertheless retain their apartments in the successor states of the former Soviet Union. Members of the Palestinian diaspora in refugee camps in Lebanon and Syria, deprived of the right to qualify for citizenship in these countries, cherish

the prospect of returning one day to the homes that their grandparents left behind in 1948 and 1967. They monitor events closely in Israel, the Occupied Territories, and the Palestine Authority. Overseas Chinese extended families, whose members are located in the capital cities of several southeast Asian states, operate the several Chinese multinational commercial, financial, and manufacturing firms that dominate the indigenous private sector in that region.[4] Their operations extend beyond their region to south Asia and the Americas.

2. *Diasporas may attempt by direct action to influence events in their country of origin.* Such attempted interventions may be in support of or in opposition to its current government. These interventions may involve the supply of weapons, combat personnel, money, or specialized expertise. Overseas Chinese financed the rebellion in 1911 that overthrew the sclerotic Imperial C'hing regime which had ruled China for two and a half centuries, and inaugurated the republican government of Dr Sun Yat-sen. From the safety of their host country, diasporas sustain conflicts in their erstwhile homeland, often supporting the most extreme elements in their homeland's politics, while those who face the reality of conflict are more willing to compromise in order to end the mayhem and destruction.

Funds from the Tamil diaspora in Britain, Canada, and the United States, some extorted by militant activists from well-to-do Tamils, are believed to finance the purchase of weapons for the insurgent Liberation Tigers of Tamil Eelam in Sri Lanka's endless civil war. In addition, these remittances maintain consumption levels among the civilian population in the territories controlled by the Tigers, relieving the Tigers of the burden of providing for their civilians. International mediation to achieve a compromise settlement of this bloody conflict has failed. Because of the brutal methods they employ, including the conscription of children, the United States and other western states have branded the Tigers a terrorist organization. This is an example of a diaspora supporting an armed revolt in its homeland by ethnic militants against an internationally recognized state.

The Armenian diaspora in France and California helps finance the military activities of the embattled republic of Armenia, including the construction of a modern highway connecting the republic, over Azerbaijan territory, with the majority Armenian enclave of Nagorno-Karabakh, which is totally surrounded by Azerbaijan. With the demise of Yugoslavia in 1991, Croatian- and Serbian-Americans furnished funds and volunteers that assisted their respective newly independent homelands in their wars over territory in Krajina and Bosnia. This bloody conflict was not terminated until the Dayton Agreement hosted by US President Clinton in 1995.[5]

Opposing factions in a diaspora community may support different parties in their homeland. For several decades, overseas Chinese were divided in their sympathies and in their support, moral and financial, between the communist and nationalist contenders for control of their former homeland. With US recognition of the communist regime in 1972, this conflict was terminated. Since the end of the Maoist era in the late 1970s, overseas Chinese capitalists have become the largest investors in China's industrial modernization.[6] Members of the Palestinian diaspora in Kuwait and other Middle East countries supplied funds and "volunteers" to participate in the PLO's operations against Israel, and charitable funds to assist their hard-pressed countrymen in the occupied West Bank and Gaza. Some channeled funds and provided fighters for the secular nationalist Fatah faction; others supported their Islamist opponents in the Hamas faction. The several competing factions within the Zionist movement in the United States provide election specialists and campaign funds to their counterpart faction within Israel, with the intention of influencing election outcomes. Prominent Israeli politicians visit the United States to stimulate fund raising for their faction prior to election campaigns.

These activities can prove a source of embarrassment to the host country's government. A militant faction of the

Irish-American diaspora supplied weapons clandestinely to the Irish Republican Army, which had been branded a terrorist organization and was conducting lethal terrorist operations in London and other British cities in their campaign to force the British to leave Northern Ireland. Washington's closest European ally believed the United States government could and should have done more to block the flow of these weapons. After 9/11, the US government embargoed the flow of "charitable" contributions from Arab-Americans to Middle East organizations suspected of terrorist connections.

3. *Diasporas attempt to influence their host government or international organizations to act in favor of or in opposition to the interests of the current government of their home country.* Several diaspora communities in the United States maintain offices in Washington to track events in the US government that might be favorable or unfavorable to the interests of their constituents in the United States as well as their former homeland. They are prepared to intervene or to activate their diaspora community politically when these interests appear to be threatened by congressional action or by decisions taken in the executive agencies. The Cuban diaspora in the United States has for several decades successfully urged Washington to maintain a hard line against the communist Castro regime in Cuba, including an economic embargo. The dominant faction of Cuban-Americans in Florida continues to promote this hard line, while a minority faction urges, so far unsuccessfully, a more flexible policy, arguing that US trade, investment, and tourism would benefit the Cuban people, while undermining the Castro regime.[7]

The Palestinian diaspora, along with Arab and Muslim states, has since 1967 persuaded the United Nations General Assembly in its annual meetings to condemn Israel's occupation of the West Bank and Gaza and to brand Israel an international pariah, a violator of UN resolutions, and a "racist" society. The Armenian diaspora has pressured the World Bank to increase its assistance to the republic of Armenia.

Diasporas normally retain affectionate sentiments toward their erstwhile homeland and are disposed to be helpful when this is possible. In addition to remittances of funds to families and local communities, members of diasporas, when they are financially able, provide direct investments and technical assistance in support of the economic development of their former homelands. The industrial development agencies of homeland governments actively solicit their support and participation. As noted previously, overseas Chinese capitalists have become major investors in the industrial modernization of post-Maoist China, their familiarity with the language and local business practices yielding them competitive advantages over Japanese and western firms. Members of the Indian diaspora in North America have assisted Indian firms in the information technology sector to establish linkages with American companies interested in establishing beachheads in India's expanding computer industry.[8]

Diasporas wish to be helpful to their former homeland, while at the same time demonstrating their compatibility with the interests of their host country. Jews in the diaspora are concerned that no harm should come to independent Israel, which they view as the fulfillment of the millennial aspiration of their ancestors and which must continue to be available as a national refuge for Jews who suffer persecution in the diaspora. Those in the United States consider themselves patriotic Americans who view their love for Israel as completely consistent with America's national interest. They argue that, as the sole democracy in the Middle East, Israel is the only reliable ally of the United States in that region of the world. Yet, its very existence is threatened by Arab-Muslim enemies, some of which are hosts to terrorist organizations that intend harm to the United States. Therefore, it is in America's national security interest to provide consistent and generous diplomatic, economic, and military assistance to Israel, a position that has won the support of the US government and of a large majority of the American public.

German-Americans who attempted to prevent the United States from entering the two world wars against their former homeland argued, unsuccessfully, that it was in the United States' national interest to stay out of Europe's wars.

Among Israel's most fervent supporters in the United States are Evangelical Christians, who happen to comprise the core of the contemporary Republican Party. They believe that the restoration of the Israeli state from the ashes of the Holocaust constitutes a divinely inspired miracle that heralds the reuniting of all Jews in Jerusalem, their Holy City, and their subsequent conversion to Christianity. This, they believe, is a necessary prelude to the second coming of Christ and the inauguration of the Messianic era, the end of days. Despite its many factions, the American-Jewish diaspora has operated an effective informational and lobbying organization that has attempted, successfully, to project a favorable image of Israel as a reliable, democratic ally and to fend off criticism from unfriendly sources.

The American-Jewish lobby is but one of numerous similar operations that seek to influence the diplomatic, economic, and security policies of the US government in relation to their erstwhile homelands. They too argue that support for their homeland – Ukraine, Poland, Morocco, the Philippines, Pakistan, Taiwan – is not only morally sound, but entirely compatible with American national interest.

4. *Home governments attempt to use their diaspora to support their strategic or economic goals.* Most commonly, they establish banking and related facilities to enhance the flow of financial remittances from members of their diaspora to families and friends back home. Financial remittances constitute valuable supplements to national foreign exchange earnings. In the aggregate, remittances of funds from members of diasporas to families, friends, and communities in their homelands totaled more than $300 billion in 2006, double the flow of foreign aid to less developed countries.[9] Mexico, for example, nets $20 billion annually from its diaspora in the United States. A unit in its Foreign Office services the needs of its American diaspora, whose members are encouraged to visit the homeland and spend generously as tourists. As

members of the diaspora are permitted to vote in Mexico's elections, candidates for office actively campaign among Mexican-Americans for their votes.

Several countries, notably Korea, China, and India, attempt to reverse the brain drain by luring members of their diaspora who have achieved skills and experience in high-level scientific and technological employment to return to their former homeland and contribute knowledge acquired in the diaspora to its industrial, educational, medical, or military modernization. Korea has established a high-level scientific research organization, the Korean Advanced Institute for Science and Technology (KAIST), staffed mainly by returnees from its large American diaspora. Returnees are promised salaries comparable to their earnings in the United States and laboratory facilities that enable them to sustain their research programs.[10]

During World War I, the imperial government of Germany attempted to prevent the United States from entering the war on the side of the allied powers, Britain and France. At that time the German diaspora in the US was the largest and best organized ethnic community in the country. The German foreign office provided leaders and publications of the German-American community with propaganda themes. It urged German-American business leaders, clergymen, and politicians to use their considerable influence with members of Congress to maintain American neutrality and stay out of Europe's war. It advised German-American community leaders to form a political coalition with the politically powerful Irish-American community, who opposed any assistance to their British enemy. As it turned out, the German-American mobilization failed and the German government was accused of unwarranted interference in America's internal affairs. Despite Berlin's best efforts, the US entered the war on the side of the Allies. Following Japan's invasion of China in the 1930s, China's government urged Chinese merchants in southeast Asia to boycott Japanese merchandise. The Chinese diaspora responded favorably, and the boycott was enforced by Chinese secret societies.

To cite a more recent example of a government's efforts to manipulate its diaspora: the Israeli government actively inspires American-Jewish organizations to pressure members of Congress to continue and even increase its diplomatic, military, and financial support for Israel's defense against hostile forces in the Middle East.

5. *A hard-pressed diaspora may seek protection from its home government.* When members of the Chinese diaspora in Vietnam during the late 1970s were harassed by the Vietnamese government, fresh from its victory over the Americans, the People's Republic was not satisfied with protesting. It launched a punitive military expedition against Vietnam "to teach them a lesson." This, however, was a rare occurrence. When diasporas turn to their home country for assistance, they normally find themselves orphaned. The foreign policy requirements of governments trump obligations to their diasporas. As long as China's government clung to the principle of *ius sanguinis*, ethnic Chinese, wherever they happened to be, remained Chinese subjects, and thus responsibilities of the Chinese government. Chinese diasporas might expect a sympathetic response to requests for assistance. But after 1978, when Beijing began to emphasize a policy of friendly relations with southeast Asian governments, it abandoned the principle of *ius sanguinis* in favor of *ius soli*, that persons, whatever their ethnic background, are subject to the laws of their country of residence. Overseas Chinese were advised by Beijing to become good citizens of their new country. The diaspora could no longer expect intervention from its former homeland. In 1997–8, when Chinese in Indonesia suffered a pogrom at the hands of Indonesian mobs, there was no help from Beijing.

Similarly, when the Indian diaspora in Uganda was despoiled of its property and summarily deported, it turned in vain for help from its homeland. The government of India considered it more important to adhere to its anti-colonial posture of non-interference in the sovereignty of other states, than to respond to pleas for help from its oppressed diaspora.[11] Just as reluctant homelands may decline to help a distressed diaspora, a diaspora may decline to respond to requests for support from its homeland. During World War II, Nazi Germany attempted to induce the German-American diaspora to refuse to cooperate with US war mobilization. With few exceptions, German-Americans valued their US citizenship above their residual affection for their former homeland.

6. *A host government may call on a resident diaspora to support its strategic or economic goals.* To demonstrate its patriotism and its loyalty to its host country, members of a diaspora may be more than willing to comply. In the critical 1948 Italian elections, US government officials asked Italian-Americans to contact family and friends in their former homeland, urging them to cast their votes for anti-Communist candidates. This campaign was successful in turning back the Communist challenge to Italy's fledgling post-fascist and pro-western regime. Malaysia's government arranged for its Chinese diaspora to use its contacts to facilitate the flow of exports, particularly rubber and palm oil, to the expanding Chinese market. During its second Iraq campaign beginning in 2003, the US military recruited urgently needed interpreters and translators from the ranks of the Arab-American diaspora.

As these examples indicate, a diaspora may prove to be an asset to its host country in its external strategic and economic relations. On the other hand, its members may be suspected of dual loyalty and even of disloyalty during crisis situations. During World War I, young Ukrainian-Canadian males were rounded up as enemy aliens, incarcerated in concentration camps, and subjected to hard labor on infrastructure projects, even though they had no sentimental attachment to Austria-Hungary, a country at war with Canada. The Japanese diaspora in the US was "relocated" to concentration camps during the Pacific War, though there had not been a single case of subversion or disloyalty on their part. Following terrorist incidents in Britain in 2006 and 2007, members of its Pakistani diaspora were suspected of providing aid and comfort to terrorist conspirators within its ranks. The latter are believed to accept instructions from terrorist organizations based in their homeland. The 400,000-strong Palestinian diaspora was summarily expelled from Kuwait for allegedly sympathizing with Iraqi invaders during the Gulf War.

7. *Diasporas contribute to the political, educational, and economic development of their former homeland.* The provision of such assistance depends on the capabilities of members of the diaspora community, their inclination, and the willingness and ability of the home government to receive such assistance. We have noted the contribution of overseas Chinese capitalists to China's recent industrial growth, and of information specialists in the US-based Indian diaspora to the explosive expansion of India's software industry. The principal infrastructure of Israel's impressive universities has been financed by members of the Jewish diaspora. Virtually every building is named for a North American Jewish donor. Israel's universities maintain offices in North America for fundraising purposes. On the other hand, aside from generous charitable contributions, the Armenian diaspora has been disinclined to invest in Armenia's economy because of a negative business climate.

During the Soviet occupation, the diasporas of the "captive nations" in eastern Europe were unable to provide democratic assistance, even during the brief Helsinki thaw in the 1970s and *glasnost* in the 1980s. But once the iron curtain was lifted, they eagerly assisted. Working with local counterparts, political scientists drafted new constitutions and election laws, lawyers worked to reform the Soviet-style judiciary, journalists fostered a free press, economists spurred reforms in the direction of market economies. Some of the democratic reformers stayed only briefly; others remained to help implement the reforms they had participated in drafting.

8. *The home government may request the host government to restrain hostile acts by members of the latter's diaspora community.* Ankara has asked Berlin to block the flow of funds and

weapons from its Kurdish diaspora to Kurdish insurgents in southeast Turkey. Sri Lanka has asked Britain to block the flow of funds from its Tamil diaspora to Tamil insurgents in Sri Lanka's civil war. Britain urged Washington to block the flow of funds and weapons by elements of the Irish-American diaspora to the Irish Republican Army. Such requests are seldom successful in producing favorable responses, unless these diaspora communities are also seen to be threatening the security of their host country. In these cases there was no such concern.

9. *The current threat of violent attacks by elements of terrorist organizations, many associated and inspired by Al Qaeda, has cast suspicion on several diaspora communities.* They are suspected of harboring sympathizers and participants in terrorist conspiracies and operations, such as the 9/11 attacks on New York and Washington, subsequent lethal operations in London and Madrid, assassinations in Amsterdam, and threats to publishers in Copenhagen. Every European and North American country has adopted protective measures that focus special attention, including intelligence and police surveillance, on their Muslim diasporas.[12] Suspects, especially those found to be in the country illegally, are subject to police harassment and deportation. Spokespersons for governments emphasize that these measures are not intended to disparage Islam or to disturb law-abiding members of diasporas, but are necessary to anticipate and prevent criminal attacks by rogue members of these communities.

Most terrorist operations are believed, by western intelligence specialists, to be plotted and supervised by transnational organizations that provide doctrine, training, supplies, funding, and cover to local activists. Among them are the suicide bombers who commit most of the actual terrorist crimes against American and European targets.

Beyond the transnational lifestyles of some members of diasporas, especially of the immigrant generation, diasporas may, as this chapter demonstrates, become significant actors in international affairs. They may also be treated as resources to be activated and deployed to further their strategic or economic ends either by host governments, by their former home governments, or by opposition factions operating from their former homeland. At the same time, factions of some diasporas may be suspected of hostility to their host country, or of having sympathy with and offering assistance to their host country's enemies, including terrorist organizations. They are subjected, like elements of the Pakistani diaspora in Britain, to special intelligence and police surveillance.

6

Diasporas and ethnic conflict

Ethnic conflicts are disputes between two or more ethnic communities or between one or more such communities and governments.[1] Diasporas are likely to generate conflicts because of the threats they represent to elements of the local society. Governments have the dual and often conflicting responsibilities of satisfying the demands of domestic constituencies, while attempting to manage conflicts between these constituents and diaspora communities.

The subjects of these disputes may be *political*: claims for possession of the same territory, terms and conditions for participation in government, including access to citizenship, voting rights and office-holding, election results, eligibility for public services, or collective self-determination – the right to remain a separate community; *cultural*: the rights and status of minority languages and religions, or perceived denial of respect for a community and its culture; or *economic*: unequal access or denial of access to education, employment, housing, capital, credit, and business opportunities. Disputes over any of these issues may be waged peacefully, within existing political institutions and practices; or they may erupt into violence, terrorist acts, guerilla warfare, even civil war. Such conflicts may be state-wide in scale, or confined to particular localities. Violence is usually precipitated by a minority of community activists, many members remaining on the sidelines as observers, sympathizers, victims, or skeptics and opponents of the initiatives of activists speaking in their name.

There are two principal sources of ethnic conflict: disaffected homeland communities that have occupied the same territory for long periods of time, and immigrant diasporas.

Disaffected homeland communities

Homeland communities may clash when two or more find themselves within the same state boundaries under the same political authority, as a consequence of war, conquest, or the redrawing of state boundaries. For example, the creation of the state of Belgium in 1830 incorporated the anti-clerical French-speaking Walloons and the devoutly Catholic Dutch-speaking Flemings under the same political roof. Political conflict, waged peacefully, between these two communities continues nearly two centuries later, and Belgium may not survive as a bi-national state. As the Chinese empire, the self-styled Middle Kingdom, expanded, it brought into its realm such "barbarian" peoples as Tibetans and Uighurs, who resented the loss of their freedom and were disinclined to accept the laws and the culture of Han (mainstream Chinese) civilization. They particularly resented the colonization of their homeland by Chinese. They remain part of the People's Republic only by police and military coercion. A disputed presidential election in Kenya in December 2007 ignited violence between the Kikuyu people and members of the Luo–Kalenjin coalition. This brutal ethnic conflict claimed 800 lives, left 250,000 families homeless, caused billions of dollars in property damage, and totally disrupted economic activity for two months.

After the collapse of the multinational Ottoman Empire, the British occupation authority created the state of Mesopotamia (later, Iraq), which brought the majority Arabs and the minority Kurds and Turkmen under the same government, with the Arabs in turn split between the mutually hostile Shi'a and Sunni sects. The American occupation authorities are now (2008) embroiled in a violent struggle for control of the Iraqi state. Grievances between homeland communities and governments produce ethnic conflicts. Much of the scholarship on ethnic conflict has focused on disputes involving homeland peoples.

Ethnic nationalism served as the principal ideological foundation of nineteenth- and twentieth-century states. The ethnic nation has been perceived as the appropriate political community for the modern state. The state is expected to serve, in turn, as the homeland and political expression of that community. Germany has been the state of the German nation, Hungary of the Magyar people, France of the French, Japan of the Yamato race, etc. Outsiders were welcome to the nation's territory only as temporary resident guests, as diplomats, students, entrepreneurs, or workers. They were expected to depart when their work was done. Those allowed to remain permanently were expected to adopt the mainstream culture and join the national mainstream as quickly as possible. Where historically two or more peoples were located within the state's borders, as in Nigeria, India, and Turkey, this was regarded as an anomaly of history that had to be skillfully managed, lived with, or, better still, ended. Thus, Norwegians were allowed to separate peacefully from Sweden in 1909 and Slovaks from Czech-dominated Czechoslovakia in 1993. After a bloody rebellion, in 1922 Ireland (minus its six northern counties) finally gained its independence from Britain. In 1971, Bengali East Pakistan revolted against Punjabi-dominated West Pakistan and, with the help of India, achieved its independence from Pakistan as Bangladesh.

Diasporas and the indigenous majority

Given this spirit of ethno-nationalism, immigrant communities, diasporas, that moved into the territory of an established nation were certain to be regarded with suspicion. Contacts between these diasporas and members of the established nation and their governments are the second source of contemporary ethnic conflict and the one that concerns us in this study. Though they may be needed for their labor or economic skills, or tolerated as hapless refugees from war or oppression, the mere presence of these immigrant communities can be offensive, even threatening, to members of the indigenous majority. Encountering an unintelligible foreign language in public places and witnessing the proliferation of foreign-language signs on the shops of business enterprises raise troubling questions: what are these foreigners doing in our country? Are they taking over our country? Why can't they at least learn our language and try to do things the way we do them?

Then comes the competition. Taking over scarce low-income housing, forcing up rents, encroaching on neighborhoods; "stealing" jobs from native workers by accepting slave wages and undercutting labor standards; abusing public services – health clinics, hospitals, welfare and unemployment payments, financed by taxes extracted from hard-working native taxpayers; overwhelming public schools with children who cannot speak the native language. Rumors circulate that these foreigners, unclean and racially diverse, spread diseases and engage in criminal activities. Polls indicate that substantial majorities, especially among the working class that has most contact with them, believe there are already too many immigrants in the country, that government should embargo further immigration and reduce the number already in the country.

These grievances soon reach the public agenda and are politicized by ambitious spokespersons who build political careers around hostility to immigrants and demands that their numbers be reduced and their activities circumscribed by law and administrative action. Their hostility is focused on all immigrants, especially those who have entered the country illegally or have overstayed their visas. Le Pen in France, Powell in Britain, Buchanan in the United States, Haidar in Austria, are prominent politicians of this ilk. Appealing to angry and frightened local nativists, they demonize immigrants as disease-spreading criminals, as racially and culturally inassimilable outsiders who endanger the cultural and political integrity of the nation. To preempt their appeal, mainstream parties, especially those to the right of center, such as Sarkozy in France, Thatcher in Britain, and US Republican presidential candidates in 2008 incorporate anti-immigrant themes into their programs.

Thus, the fate of diasporas, their status, security, rights, and opportunities to gain citizenship, become contentious issues on the agendas of governments. Employers who have come to depend on immigrant labor, including illegals, use their considerable political influence at local as well as national levels, often successfully, to neutralize hostility to immigrant workers and their families, and mitigate enforcement of anti-immigrant laws and policies. They are joined in unlikely coalitions by religious, humanitarian, and civil liberties NGOs that provide political support, legal assistance, and subsistence to embattled immigrants. Among those who have entered the country illegally, their locally born children may, *ipso facto*, be citizens of their host country. Yet, their parents, as violators of the law, are threatened with deportation.

Immigrants may be victimized by natives, projecting their anger and frustrations on defenseless foreigners in their midst. In post-apartheid South Africa, a minority of Africans have prospered, but a large number, estimated at 40 percent, have experienced unemployment, landlessness, and economic privation. At the same time, large numbers of immigrants from economically depressed neighbors, Zimbabwe, Malawi, and Mozambique, have moved to South Africa to participate in its relative prosperity. In 2008 they comprised 9 percent of South Africa's population. Many have found employment, undercutting local wage rates and labor standards, while entrepreneurs have set up and operated competitive retail stores. During May 2008, in the townships outside Johannesburg, native mobs went on a rampage. Blaming foreigners for their economic hardships, they looted and destroyed shops operated by immigrants, burned their homes, and slaughtered helpless men, women, and children. By the time police finally intervened, an estimated 42 "foreigners" had been brutally murdered, entire settlements razed, and communities terrorized. Estimates of the homeless ranged from 13,000 to 20,000. Busloads of destitute, demoralized immigrants are returning to their home country.[2] The diasporas served as convenient scapegoats for the economic woes suffered by indigenous inhabitants.

Grievances among diasporas

Grievances within diaspora communities usually originate with members of the second generation. Locally born and reared, they develop expectations to be respected and treated like ethnic natives. When they discover that their inherited culture and religion are demeaned, that employment and career opportunities are blocked by discrimination, when their very presence evokes harassment by the authorities, the seeds of frustration and resentment have been sown. Among the second and third generations of labor diasporas, these grievances may be expressed in delinquent behavior, in street crime, in refusal to identify with mainstream culture or to accept mainstream citizenship, and in extreme cases, by participation in subversive organizations. As their behavior draws attention by the police and the courts, and more of their members populate local prisons, their grievances culminate in chronic criminal violence against what they perceive as mainstream targets. On occasions, their frustrations may erupt into violent protest, as with north Africans in France in 2005 and Afro-Caribbeans in Britain during the 1990s.

Entrepreneurial diasporas, sensing discrimination in educational institutions, in membership in the learned professions, and in obtaining credit and business licenses, respond not by violence, but by probing for special niches or high-risk businesses that have been avoided by mainstream professionals and entrepreneurs. Thus, in East Coast cities in the United States, Korean entrepreneurs gained control of wholesale and retail fruit and vegetable marketing, Jews pioneered and developed the ready-to-wear fashion industry, and German entrepreneurs became the nation's brewers.

Localized grievances that alienate youthful, second-generation male Muslim members of labor diasporas from the governments and societies of their European host country include the absence of decent jobs, victimization by landlords, and harassment by police. These local frustrations are magnified by such national measures as crackdowns on illegal immigrants, denying Muslim girls the right to wear headscarves in school, and allowing criticism and ridicule of the prophet, Mohammad, to go unrebuked and unpunished. On the international level, the unwillingness of the government of their host country to at least protest repeated atrocities against innocent Muslims in Chechnya, Kashmir, and especially Palestine means that by inaction it has become complicit in the persecution of Muslims. Such examples of hostility at all levels of government convince them of an unrelieved anti-Muslim bias. The duty to respond to this predicament of Muslims under siege has become the major recruiting theme for young *jihadists* throughout Europe.[3]

The role of the state

The modern state is a central player in every manifestation of ethnic conflict. In referring to "the state," I recognize that governments, like the societies they represent and like diaspora communities, are seldom monolithic. They may contain agencies, such as the police and border control departments, that emphasize strict enforcement of the law, while the professional ethics and orientation of educators, doctors, and social workers stretch their interpretation of laws and policies, allowing them to provide services sympathetically to immigrants and their families, legal and illegal. The executive branch of government may propose one policy, while the legislature insists on another. US President George W. Bush in 2007 proposed and supported legislation that would have afforded some undocumented workers a path to legal status and eventual American citizenship. This proposal was blocked in Congress by an angry nativist faction, concerned that it would grant "amnesty" to law-breakers. Lurking beneath the surface of that opposition was unmistakable racist animus against dark-skinned foreigners.

The state determines, often after contentious debate, which outsiders may legally enter its territory and under what conditions they may remain. Its police patrol its borders to deter illegal immigration; they pursue individuals who are found to have entered the country illegally or to have over-stayed the terms of their original admission. The police tangle with gangs of immigrant and embittered, alienated second-generation youth whom they suspect of criminal activities. Clashes between police and diaspora youth accentuate the grievances that precipitate violent outbreaks. The sustained violence that broke out in the Paris suburbs and other French cities in the fall of 2005, as described in section 3a of chapter 3, serves as a classic but by no means unique example of this kind of conflict.

Members of low-income labor diasporas draw heavily on the health and welfare services of governments. They utilize its unemployment compensation, child allowances, and social security provisions, and send their children to public schools. Though the services available to diaspora communities tend to be inferior to those available to the native middle class, they are usually far superior to those in their former homeland. Because many members of diaspora communities neither speak nor understand the national language, these agencies are compelled to equip themselves at additional cost to handle the local workload in a second, unfamiliar language. Throughout contemporary Europe, diasporas are accused of overwhelming local public services that are financed by hard-working, over-burdened native taxpayers. Measures are proposed, as in California in 1994, to deny public services, including schooling, to illegal immigrants and their children. Bilingual education, mandated by US Federal law, has become a source of controversy in areas with large immigrant populations. In retaliation, many states and localities have declared English to be their (sole) official language and failed to provide bilingual schooling. As hosts to large labor diasporas from labor-surplus Muslim countries, contemporary European governments are wrestling with measures to deal with diasporas that show few signs of wishing to integrate into their societies and, in addition, are suspected of harboring terrorists.

Unwelcome immigrants

The unwelcome presence of immigrants, especially immigrants of exotic ethnicity and religion, may precipitate ethnic violence. Assam, a state in northeastern India, has been the scene of uninterrupted conflict among its several indigenous ethnic communities. It has also witnessed a half-century of violence directed by members of the native Assamese Hindu majority against impoverished Muslim immigrants from overpopulated neighboring Bangladesh, who spill over the border in search of work. As their numbers grew to three million, more than 10 percent of Assam's population, Assamese natives feared that their lands, their jobs, even control of their country were threatened by the economically more aggressive Muslim Bangladeshi invaders, whose birth rate, they believe, is much higher than that of Assamese natives. Led by the militant All-Assam Students Union, violence flares periodically against Bangladeshi immigrants, forcing many thousands to abandon their lands, their jobs, and their homes to seek protection across the border. After the dead have been buried and the dust has settled from these periodic violent episodes, Bangladeshi immigrants begin once again to trickle back into Assam, arriving at times at the rate of 6,000 a day, escaping the desperate landlessness, joblessness, and poverty of their homeland. The persistent presence of this ethnically and religiously foreign diaspora has become a chronic irritant and a repeated source of violent conflict in northeastern India.[4]

Because of its dynamic economy, Malaysia suffers chronic labor shortages. It has recently attracted an estimated three million immigrants, half of them believed to be illegals from neighboring labor-surplus countries, Indonesia, Bangladesh,

Philippines, Myanmar, and Vietnam. For more than a decade, Malaysia's government has sought ways to cope with this flood of illegals, who are welcome and appreciated by employers, but denounced by government officials as law-breakers. The government has therefore deputized a half-million civilian volunteers to ferret out, identify, and arrest illegal immigrants and turn them over to government officials. If judged to be illegally in the country, these immigrants are subject to imprisonment, whippings, and deportation.[5] The government-sponsored vigilante organization, the People's Volunteer Corps, appears to be a cost-effective supplement to its system of law enforcement. In November 2007, it claimed credit for stopping and searching 156,000 persons who appeared to be Asian foreigners and identifying 30,000 who could not present proper documentation. Since as many as half these volunteers have not been trained, there have been frequent reports of abuse of their authority, including beatings, thefts, extortion of money and valuables, and violent disruption of living quarters. As in other countries, illegal immigrants, useful for their labor, are vulnerable to official harassment, suspected of committing crimes and spreading diseases. Nativist volunteers in the United States, self-styled "minutemen," have supplemented the government's border control agents, patrolling the porous boundary between Mexico and Arizona for illegal immigrants.[6]

Managing ethnic conflict

As foreigners in their midst, diasporas are likely to generate conflict with members of the indigenous society. Governments, in turn, are expected to manage these conflicts by implementing strategies that regulate the status of the diaspora and its members in relation to the state and to mainstream society. There are three strategies by which states attempt to manage these relationships.

The first is by *maintaining and enforcing pluralism*. This strategy may reflect agreement among the communities that they desire to remain separate and distinct. Malays and Chinese in Malaysia, Jews and Palestinians in Israel, and Germans and Turks in Bavaria are examples of communities in the same state that desire to maintain their separate collective identities. But though the parties may agree to remain separate, they may disagree on the terms of their relationship. One community, usually the indigenous, remains politically superior, its government imposing and enforcing this superior/subordinate relationship on the other. Even, for example, if the minority Chinese should agree to convert to Islam and be absorbed into the Malay community, they would still not be recognized as *bumiputera* (native sons), and thus would not be entitled to the special privileges and first-class citizenship available to all Malays. Though Palestinians are Israeli citizens, they remain second-class citizens. Their language enjoys official status and they are guaranteed religious freedom, but they have been excluded from political power, discriminated against in government allocations, and suspected by many Israelis as a potential "fifth column," enemies within the gates.

There are policies that deny members of diasporas admittance to the mainstream and compel them to remain a separate and subordinate community. Kuwaiti elites made it clear that the Palestinian diaspora, though economically prominent and prosperous, must remain a separate community excluded from the Kuwaiti mainstream. They could not aspire to Kuwaiti citizenship. Though discrimination because of race or color is criminalized under Brazil's current constitution, Afro-Brazilians have nevertheless been excluded from Brazil's mainstream because of pervasive and persistent race prejudice. Marginalization and separation have been imposed, in this case not by government policy, but by social custom and economic discrimination, thwarting the desire of Brazil's large Afro-Brazilian minority to be accepted and incorporated into the mainstream.

The second strategy *promotes and rewards integration into the mainstream*. It permits relatively non-discriminatory access and participation by individuals in mainstream educational, occupational, economic, and political institutions on terms established by mainstream authorities. It implies the gradual atrophy and eventual disappearance of diaspora communities as individuals join the mainstream and allow their connections with diaspora institutions and culture to lapse. Unless reinforced by fresh arrivals, some diasporas sooner or later disappear. Some states, such as France, Thailand, and Israel, prescribe and promote a radical assimilationist strategy, expecting immigrants to become French, Thai, and Israeli in short order. The second generation of Russian Jews in Israel is being integrated into Israel's Jewish majority, as are Sino-Thai in Thailand. The unwillingness of France's mainstream to accept north Africans, or of members of that large diaspora to comply with France's assimilationist strategy, has created a crisis in French politics that has yet to be resolved. The US strategy favors integration. Its melting pot claims the second- and third-generation children of its diasporas, while mainstream culture accepts and incorporates as its own certain elements of their disappearing cultures.

According to the third strategy, *government and mainstream society tolerate pluralism, even respecting diversity as a short-term expedient and in some cases as a permanent arrangement.* Canada's multiculturalism celebrates and finances the maintenance and expression of its cultural diversity, contrasting its "mosaic" with the US assimilationist "melting pot." In fact, most members of Canada's diasporas, by the third generation, have joined either the English-speaking or the French-speaking mainstream. The US tolerates its many diasporas, providing even radio and TV outlets, cultural events (St Patrick's Day parades), and political outlets (Polish-American Democratic Clubs). Their members enjoy a hybrid or split identity, participating actively in mainstream institutions and adopting mainstream lifestyles, while maintaining their affiliation with the diaspora and perceiving no dissonance between these two identities. Where necessary, US practice recognizes minorities, such as Amish and Hasidic Jews, who insist on maintaining their distinctive culture and lifestyle. These are not imposed by government or mainstream society, but reflect the desire of these communities to remain separate.

Within the broad canopy of this strategy are arrangements that allow individuals to participate in the mainstream, its institutions and lifestyle, while retaining links with their diaspora. These links may be based on a distinctive religious tradition or on sentiments of political obligation or solidarity, such as the Irish struggle for independence, the Palestinian aspiration to recover their homeland, and the Armenian determination to avenge the genocide of 1915–16. For a period of time, these split or hybrid identities are accepted by their host government, as long as they steer clear of any threat to national security, with the confident expectation that mainstream attachments and the attraction of mainstream culture will eventually diminish the salience of their diaspora identity.

Managing ethnic conflicts, including those that involve diaspora communities, is mainly, but not exclusively, a responsibility of governments. The relevant governments are those within whose borders the conflicts occur. The British government has, for example, attempted to respond to the grievances of its Afro-Caribbean diaspora and of its Pakistani diaspora, while maintaining close surveillance of suspected *jihadists* among the Pakistani. Occasionally, however, foreign governments or international organizations offer their good offices as mediators. Norway's foreign office and the US Presidency have attempted to mediate the Israel–Palestine conflict. The Organization for Security and Cooperation in Europe (OCSE) intervened in Latvia and Estonia to protect the citizenship status and language rights of their Russian minorities after these countries had regained their independence following the dissolution of the Soviet Union. Non-government organizations, such as the Carter Center, attempt to contribute to the management and settlement of conflicts involving diaspora communities. The Carter Center has actively intervened in the Israeli–Palestinian conflict.

How can one evaluate the effectiveness of conflict management strategies? The short-term criterion is success in *maintaining order* by accommodating grievances through the state's political institutions and processes, or by providing avenues for achieving satisfaction despite the persistence of some grievances. These are reinforced by the ability of the state's security forces to deter violent protest. The Russian state, having failed to manage its relationships with its Chechyn minority, was forced to resort to military intervention that intensified the conflict. Conflict management failed in Malaysia in 1969 when Malays, in and around the capital city, Kuala Lumpur, feared that as a consequence of election results they might lose their dominant position in government. When the police proved unable to bring the resulting violence under control, the Malay regiment was summoned to restore order. Since then, Malays have been reassured by measures that entrench their control of government and offer them increased opportunities to participate in the modern sectors of the economy. Despite unresolved political grievances, Chinese have been mollified by opportunities for economic and occupational success. Thailand is successfully absorbing its large Chinese diaspora into its mainstream culture and society, but the Malay-Muslim minority in its southern provinces insists on maintaining its separate identity. The Thai government's gestures to appease its grievances have been met with violent rejection.

In more decentralized polities, such as the United States and Canada, local and regional authorities are responsible for the management of ethnic conflict. There may be outbreaks of sporadic violence because of the failure of these authorities to anticipate or deter protest against police harassment of diaspora youth suspected of criminal activities. Order may be disrupted by violence between elements of two ethnic communities – for example, between Mexican and African-American gangs in Los Angeles, Cuban and African-American gangs in Miami, and Afro-Caribbean and Pakistani gangs in London – contesting for control of territory for gangland criminal activities. Such failures of conflict management at the local level may occur at the same time that the opportunity structure at the national level has been expanded to accommodate the aspirations of members of the diaspora for employment and political integration. On the other hand, some local authorities, as in Japan, may assist members of diasporas, while the national government disregards their existence. Because of the United States' relatively open opportunity structure, the failure of the US Congress in late 2007 to legalize the status of undocumented immigrants and provide them with avenues for obtaining citizenship did not result in organized protest or violence.

There are many unusual and ingenious ways to manage ethnic conflict, including conflicts among diaspora communities. In New York City, which hosted successive waves of immigration in the century between 1850 and 1950, immigrants were provided with needed assistance and services less by governments than by the Democratic Party "machine" known as Tammany Hall. Tammany developed and operated a network of patron–client relationships with these immigrant ethnic communities. Their assistance – food parcels and hods of coal at Christmas time, flowers at burial ceremonies, "fixing" minor criminal offenses at the behest of distressed family members, jobs in the city government, arranging hospital admissions, and similar favors of many kinds – was doled out, all in exchange for votes at election time. These votes enabled Tammany's leaders to control city government and to provide lucrative favors – at a substantial price – for businessmen, contractors, and suppliers of goods and services to the city's government. Tammany's share of these contracts enabled its leaders to maintain their organization, while lining their own pockets.

On the question of employment, Tammany evolved a rough division of labor among the larger diaspora communities: Irish controlled the New York police and fire departments, Italians ran the city's sanitation services, Jews were the school teachers and social workers. This ethnic division of labor was never air-tight, but it served to regulate competition for the city's largesse among its main ethnic communities.[7] The system gradually broke down as reformers, representing ethnic groups and social classes that were outside Tammany's control, imposed civil service rules on the city government and exposed Tammany's gross corruption. Meanwhile, new claimants to city jobs among more recent arrivals and voters, African-Americans and Puerto Ricans, overwhelmed Tammany's ability to deliver the goods to the many claimants to its patronage.

Resolution of ethnic conflict is the ultimate criterion of success in conflict management, including those conflicts that involve diaspora communities. Expansion of the opportunity structure has enabled members of several diaspora communities in Canada and the United States to gain access to educational institutions and to achieve occupational success on a non-discriminatory basis, blunting their earlier grievances. Having acculturated to the American mainstream and risen to middle-class status, many members of these earlier immigrant diasporas, Irish, German, Italian, Jewish, Polish, have moved out of the central city and into the suburbs. The boundaries separating them from other ethnic communities and grievances against an uncaring government have been supplanted by a more optimistic sense of opportunities and appreciation of their new neighbors from other ethnic backgrounds. They are well on their way to integrating into the beckoning American mainstream, while leaving their mark on mainstream culture.

European governments, however, have realized little success in managing conflicts with their growing Muslim diasporas. An analysis of this situation can be found in chapter 7, in the section, "Europe and its Muslim diasporas."

7
Diasporas and public policy

In this chapter we analyze and evaluate the various government strategies and policies encountered in this study and the likely responses of diasporas in their host country. The objectives of public policy directed at diasporas are 1) to facilitate their adaptation in the direction of the government's preferences, toward integration, separate status, or a hybrid policy such as political integration combined with social and cultural autonomy; and 2) to prevent or, if necessary, to limit the scope and intensity of ethnic conflict. When outsiders are admitted *legally* as refugees, as workers, as technicians or professionals, what conditions do governments attach to their admission?

Governments may enunciate and practice a policy of *total exclusion*: immigrants are neither needed nor wanted. In Japan, as outlined in section 3b of chapter 3, this policy is intended to maintain a mythical racial purity and the integrity of the national culture. Students, entrepreneurs, diplomats, and skilled, high-tech individuals are admitted through time-bound visas; unless these are extended, they are expected to leave the country when their work has been completed. Those who overstay their visas are in the country illegally; when apprehended they may be prosecuted or deported. Though employers clamor for unskilled labor, there is no provision in Japan's immigration policy for admitting such personnel. When the demand nevertheless emerges for immigrant labor, as it has in Japan, willing workers are certain to find a way to enter the country clandestinely. They are recruited by labor contractors and, in most cases, protected – and exploited – by employers with the assistance of local governments and acquiescence by the police. Some governments prefer to turn a blind eye to this unpleasant reality in their midst, hoping that it will somehow go away.[1] But economic necessity trumps formal policy. Diaspora communities formed in this way exist in an underground legal and status vacuum, at the mercy of employers and with no prospect of gaining secure status in their host country.

Immigrants may be admitted for limited terms under strictly enforced contracts. This policy is practiced by the sparsely populated and undereducated petroleum economies of the Persian Gulf, where governments admit many thousands of workers with diverse skills, mostly from east and south Asia. For example, as many as 85 percent of the population of the United Arab Emirates are foreign workers.[2] These immigrants, some of them highly skilled professionals, are attracted by relatively high wages, much of which they remit to their families back home. They are kept at arm's length from local societies; permanent residence is out of the question. Unless their contracts are renewed, they are required to return to their homeland when their contracted term of service has been completed.

Governments may admit immigrants under various preferential or discretionary criteria. Canada prefers immigrants with economic skills that are needed and in short supply in their country. It also favors immigrants who bring capital of a certain amount into their country. The United States, on the other hand, grants preference to family members of persons already legally in the country. Between 1924 and 1965, the US enforced national origin quotas that preferred immigrants from northern and western Europe and discriminated against persons from southern and eastern Europe; Asians were excluded entirely. Brazil continues to prefer Europeans in order to "whiten" their population. These preferential and discriminatory policies are intended either to implement certain societal goals or to respond to labor market demands. Prior to the 1960s, Australia encouraged immigration to expand its manpower base. Under the "white Australia" policy which prevailed at that time, Europeans were preferred and Asians were excluded. This policy has since been abandoned.[3]

The lessons of the European Holocaust and the civil rights movement in the United States made it impossible for western governments any longer to maintain ethnic or racial discriminatory policies. The United States, Canada, and Australia, the major countries of immigration, scrapped their discriminatory policies and practices, opening their borders to visible immigrants from Asia, Africa, and Latin America, who now constitute major diasporas in these countries. Once immigrants are admitted, Canada encourages them to become Canadians, to learn the official language, French or English, of their province, and to qualify for Canadian citizenship. Multiculturalism enables members of diaspora communities, while qualifying for Canadian citizenship, to continue to participate in and enjoy the literary, artistic, and historical expressions of their inherited culture, including its rites and celebrations. Politically, they are Canadian, while culturally they share elements of North American and their inherited cultures.[4]

The United States and Canada now operate what can be called *open or ethnically inclusive immigration policies*, setting an overall annual ceiling for legal immigrants, and avoiding racial and ethnic preferences and discrimination. Once admitted to the US as legal immigrants, they are eligible for "green cards" that enable them to move anywhere in the country, seeking the most favorable employment opportunities. They are encouraged to learn English and, after five years of continuous residence, to apply for American citizenship. Green card holders and their families are subject to normal tax rates and are eligible for all public services. As aliens, however, they are not permitted to vote or to hold public office.

Inclusive policies may be accompanied by preferences, but these may not be based on ethnic or religious criteria. As noted earlier, the United States awards preferences to family reunions, while Canada prefers immigrants who meet its demands in critical occupational categories. Some manpower specialists in the United States argue that the US should follow Canada's more economically rational example by adjusting its immigration policies to prefer immigrants with needed entrepreneurial experience or technical skills.

The problem of illegals

What rights and privileges should be accorded to illegal aliens, to individuals who slip into a country in violation of its immigration laws, find work, acquire property, marry and, in many cases, raise children who are automatically citizens by birth, while their parents, if apprehended by the authorities, are subject to summary deportation? Should their children be entitled to public education? Should illegal immigrants be permitted to obtain insurance and drivers' licenses? When the numbers of the undocumented climb into the millions, as they have in the United States, and some important industries depend on their labor, the question of their status becomes a major issue of public policy. Too numerous to be hunted down and expelled en masse as law-breakers, should they be rewarded with a form of amnesty that opens paths for legalization and eventual citizenship? Would this policy reward and encourage law breaking? Or, should they continue indefinitely in legal limbo, as outlaws who nevertheless find employment, pay taxes, and utilize the medical, health, and other tax-supported welfare services of government. When they join the military, should they be awarded citizenship at the conclusion of their term of enlistment?

Sooner rather than later, their status must be regulated. It would be unacceptable to have large, permanent contingents of individuals living and working in the country, but devoid of rights or legal status. If they first register with the authorities, pay a fine for having violated the law, thus legalizing their status, should they then receive a green card that entitles them to permanent residence and access to the normal range of public services? Employers would be required to urge their employees to register. Those who fail to do so would then be vulnerable to apprehension by reinforced immigration police and deported along with those convicted of criminal offenses.

Where the demand for labor exceeds the available supply, or where employers prefer immigrant labor to local workers, persons from labor-surplus regions find ways to enter the country. They blend into existing diaspora communities, protected by relatives or friends, find work, and join the ranks of illegal or "undocumented" immigrants. Because they are law-breakers, having entered the country as violators of its immigration laws, formal public policy calls for them to be hunted down and deported. Informally, however, because their labor is valued by employers and because they attract the sympathy of fellow ethnics and of human rights activists, enforcement of immigration laws in their cases is often lax and sporadic, allowing them to remain in the country indefinitely, but in legal and status limbo. Local communities debate the eligibility of these foreigners for public services, including healthcare and welfare payments, and the right of their children to public education.

Summary deportation of illegals is applauded by nativists, but resisted by sympathetic religious and civil rights organizations, with the tacit support of employers, as a violation of the human rights of individuals to move freely in the peaceful search for improved livelihoods. Recognizing the disruptive effects of mass deportations, governments may seek to regularize the status of long-serving illegals by offering them pathways to eventual citizenship. In the struggle to control public policy on this issue, nativists attack such initiatives as "amnesty" for law-breakers, insisting that applicable laws be strictly enforced. During June 2007, an effort by President Bush and the Democratic majority in the US Congress to enact a measure that would have enabled some undocumented workers to gain legal status was blocked by a determined minority of Senate Republicans, responding to the concerns of their nativist constituents. Ethnic conflict between Latinos, mostly Mexican-Americans, and their supporters who favored the Bush proposal, on the one hand, and nativists, who opposed "amnesty," on the other, took center stage in the struggle to control public policy.

Europe and its Muslim diasporas

The acute need for labor during the rapid post-World War II expansion of Europe's economies created an environment in which labor market requirements controlled public policy toward immigration. Recruited in most cases from labor-surplus Islamic societies in north Africa, the Middle East, and south Asia, these immigrant workers were expected to return to their homelands when their labor was no longer needed in their European host countries. Expanding on our discussion in chapter 4, two decades later, after labor markets had stabilized and in some cases contracted, and as further immigration was curtailed, these countries found themselves confronted with diasporas of visible immigrants, with exotic speech and religious cultures. Instead of returning to their homelands, as their hosts had originally expected, the great majority chose to remain in their host country. As legal immigrants, they and their families benefited from generous welfare payments when work was no longer available. The commitment of European nations to human rights precluded deporting them en masse.

As their labor continued to be needed in some sectors of European economies, they could be tolerated as long as they remained quietly in their ghettos. Their locally born, locally reared and locally educated offspring who qualified by virtue of their local birth for citizenship in several European countries were divided. A minority struggled to be integrated and accepted into the national mainstream, but the majority, sensing a hostile social environment and discriminatory local opportunity structure, declined to abandon their inherited identity, refusing even to attempt integration. A few were so alienated and embittered by what they perceived as discrimination in the labor market, chronic unemployment, absence of respect for their religion and culture, and an aggressively hostile police presence that, though personally non-observant, they joined Wahabist- and Salafist-inspired Islamist organizations. A few abetted and participated in terrorist operations. This is the societal and political reality that now confronts public policy in European countries.

The scope for public policy among European countries has been constrained by 1) continuing need for the labor of many immigrants and their children, 2) the hostility of large sectors of the native citizenry, creating an unfriendly and discriminatory opportunity structure for members of these diasporas, and 3) the limited inclination of the majority of diaspora members to integrate into the local society: limited interest in integration, reinforced by a resistant opportunity structure. Right-wing politicians build careers on "toughness" toward immigrants, who are blamed for multiple offenses such as drug trafficking and other crimes, as carriers of AIDS and other diseases, as abusers of women, and as shameless exploiters of tax-supported public services. They are accused of encroachment on working-class neighborhoods and housing, of competing unfairly for jobs, of unscrupulous business practices, of proneness to violence, and of disinterest in integrating into the national mainstream. European nativists demand that the right of immigrants to qualify for citizenship be curtailed and that immigrant law-breakers be summarily deported. Most Europeans believe their nation is and should continue to be composed of Caucasians like themselves, supported by a historically Christian culture, even though their societies have been largely secularized. That their nation may be diluted by an influx of racially and culturally diverse neighbors confronts them with an uncomfortable prospect.

The hostile opportunity structure that they encounter has generated alienation and disaffection among large segments of locally born Muslim diaspora youth, who feel the sting of discrimination and rejection, even as they are fated to remain and live their lives in Europe. Every European country, the larger ones – Britain, France, Germany, Spain – as well as their smaller neighbors – Austria, Denmark, Holland, Belgium – have been victims of terrorist incidents mounted by disaffected Muslim youth, joined by recent local converts, some apparently linked to Al Qaeda. Any criticism of their faith or of its prophet, Mohammad, evokes violent responses from alienated Muslim youth inflamed in many cases by *imams* trained in the Middle East by extremist mentors.[5]

Throughout Europe, an unlikely coalition of center-left politicians, labor unions, religious and secular humanists committed to human rights, and employers have come to the aid of immigrants, urging toleration and respect for diversity. They advocate incentives for immigrants to acculturate and participate in mainstream institutions, easing their pathway to membership in the mainstream and eventual citizenship. They work with locally born *imams* to design reforms that would adapt the practice of Islam to the democratic and secular environment of contemporary Europe. They have succeeded in incorporating some of their proposals into law, even as many of their fellow citizens remain suspicious of their Muslim neighbors.

At this juncture, it would be well to recall one of the truisms about diaspora communities: that they are never monolithic. This applies as well to the various Muslim diasporas in Europe. While many of them harbor grievances that alienate them from the authorities and societies in their host countries, others prefer to build their lives within the constraints and opportunities available to them. They master the national language, take advantage of training and educational opportunities, and gain the credentials that enable them to become entrepreneurs, skilled workers and professionals. They move out of diaspora enclaves, participate in mainstream institutions, adopt middle-class European lifestyles, and in many instances intermarry and join the national mainstream. They strive to cope with and overcome the prejudices and obstacles in their host countries to earning decent livelihoods and participating in mainstream activities, without necessarily sacrificing their religious identity as Muslims. They may continue to identify religiously as Muslims, but politically as citizens and members of the national mainstream.

Though the immigrant generation cling to their inherited culture, young, locally reared women are especially prone to acculturate to the mainstream and to take advantage of the freedoms available to women in Europe. While they share some of the frustrations and anger of their alienated compatriots, the majority of Muslims in Europe neither participate in nor sympathize with terrorist violence. They will seldom go so far, however, as to cooperate with the police to identify its perpetrators.

Some Muslim spokespersons in Europe insist that governments confer on their communities the privileges and immunities of multiculturalism, acknowledging them as separate, self-managing communities. Since they have no interest in becoming Europeans, and since Europeans reject them, separate status for Muslim diasporas, they argue, is what they mutually desire. At government expense, Muslim communities should be allowed to organize and manage their own affairs, including schools, cultural institutions, and radio and television outlets. They should have their own judicial tribunals to settle disputes among Muslims according to Islamic law (shariah). Muslims should be allocated a number of seats in local legislatures and the national parliament according to their share of the population. European states would then contain plural societies, in which Muslims and non-Muslims live their separate lives, interacting mainly in the economic sphere.

The majority of Europeans oppose separate status for Muslims in their country. Since expelling Muslims en masse would upset local labor markets and violate European principles of human rights, despite the demands of extremist politicians and pundits, it cannot be a realistic policy option. Europeans are more likely to adopt the longer-term strategy of providing incentives for individual Muslims to acculturate to their way of life, to participate in mainstream educational institutions, qualify for middle-class jobs, enjoy a middle-class European lifestyle, and adopt a national political and social identity; to become Europeans, even as they continue to adhere to a reformed version of the Muslim faith. Governments would set the pace for integration, opening the national opportunity structure to Muslims on a non-discriminatory basis, hoping that employers and others would follow the government's lead in accepting Muslims as fellow citizens, entitled to equal and respectful treatment.

Eventual integration of individual Muslims into the national mainstream, rather than conceding multicultural separation of Muslim minorities, is the preference of most Europeans and the policy they would expect their governments to implement. Since Muslims in substantial numbers are in Europe to stay, native Europeans would have to learn to accommodate some elements of the culture of their Muslim neighbors and accept visible, dark-skinned neighbors as fellow citizens. How eagerly members of the Muslim diasporas would respond to such incentives is uncertain. European governments and opinion leaders must be prepared to persevere with this effort, even in the face of initial disinterest and rejection by majorities of their Muslim diasporas, and despite sporadic protests and acts of terrorist violence perpetrated by extremists as self-appointed agents of Islam.

Separate development?

Europeans have been willing to concede autonomous, self-governing status to indigenous, territorially concentrated minorities – Scots in Britain, Catalans, Basques, and Galicians in Spain, Hungarians in Slovakia, Austrians in Italy. This form of multiculturalism can be tolerated as long as these minorities are not regarded as security risks or threaten secession. The same applies to the self-governing status conceded to First Canadians (Indian and Inuit nations) and to surviving Indian nations in the United States. The attitude toward immigrant diasporas is quite different.

Immigrant communities are not believed to be candidates for separate development or to have moral claims to such treatment. Instead, the tacit obligation of newcomers who are admitted to any country and enter it voluntarily is to conform to its national language, institutions, and way of life, while retaining, if they wish, attachment to their religious and cultural heritage. Diaspora communities that intend to remain in their adopted country, but whose members resolutely refuse to join the national mainstream and in large numbers express hostility toward their host government and society – these present European governments with an unwelcome and unprecedented predicament.[6] What should be their policy toward such communities that cannot be expelled en masse, but whose Muslim culture is believed to be incompatible with the national mainstream and some of whose members are implicated in terrorist threats to their nation's security?

Recognizing that exclusion is simply unfeasible, the prevailing sentiment in Europe is hesitant acceptance of integration as the least undesirable of available policy choices for their Muslim diasporas. No European government can be comfortable with the idea of separate, self-governing multicultural status for its Muslim minorities. They are likely to rely on patient, long-term incentives for individuals to detach themselves from their diaspora community, associate with the national mainstream, and adopt a hybrid identity that enables them to participate in the national political community, while continuing to practice their religious faith.

A straw in the wind was the set of policies enunciated in January 2008 by President Sarkozy of France, less than a year after his election on a platform that promised tough treatment of north African immigrants. As we reported in section 3a of chapter 3, he proposed a set of initiatives that would 1) provide job training for 100,000 young residents of the suburbs, 2) create "second chance" schools for former high school dropouts, 3) build new transport links enabling people in the suburbs to travel to the sites of their new jobs, 4) station 4,000 additional police officers in the suburbs to ensure security, and 5) conduct a merciless war against drug traffickers. This "Marshall Plan" for the suburbs is intended to provide a reformed and welcoming opportunity structure for north African youth, facilitating their integration into the French mainstream.

The United States, Canada, Australia and other countries built by immigrants have much smaller cohorts of Muslim diasporas. They maintain relatively open and inclusive opportunity structures that provide incentives for immigrants and their offspring to participate in mainstream institutions, accept mainstream culture, and integrate into mainstream society. This progression occurs even as second- and third-generation graduates of diasporas retain some attachments, often increasingly fragile, to their ancestral culture, especially its religious institutions. The most productive policy choices are those that call for easing the road for individual immigrants to gain membership in and identify with the mainstream, while respecting their cultural and religious heritage. Their purpose is to enable members of diasporas to gain a sense of acceptance and thus of belonging to their adopted country, while continuing to retain, if they wish, an attachment to the institutions, especially the religious institutions, of their diaspora. The process of mutual accommodation implies that while members of the diasporas adapt to the culture and institutions of their host country's mainstream, the mainstream in turn accepts as its own some symbolic elements of the diaspora culture – its popular expressions, cuisine, lifestyle.

Law and public policy

Yet, government policy does not necessarily govern their constituents' behavior. Societal behavior, more than formal policy, may shape the opportunity structures that diasporas encounter. Public policy in France has been uncompromisingly integrationist, yet the dominant public attitude toward north Africans, "Arabs," has been hostile and discriminatory. This is the image of France that most members of that diaspora encounter. Public policy in Brazil mandates equality among all Brazilians, yet white Brazilians practice a form of institutionalized racism that relegates their Afro-Brazilian compatriots to an excluded, second-class status. Even in the United States, where the law of the land and public policy proscribe racial discrimination and large-scale immigration is accepted as a feature of the national experience, a determined minority of nativists express their discomfort with Latino immigrants by insisting on rigorous enforcement of immigration laws, English only in schools and in communication with government, and restrictions on government services for illegal immigrants and their children. Labor migrants in Japan are aware not only of the national government's exclusionary policies, but also of the willingness of employers to hire them and of local governments to assist them with accommodations and with health, welfare, and educational services for them and their children.

In evaluating the opportunity structures that they encounter, members of diasporas consider less the formal structures of laws and policies, but mainly the attitudes of the public, of landlords and employers, of school teachers and police officers to the presence of "foreigners" in their midst. Public policy influences and at times determines social behavior, but there may be a large gap between government enactments and their ability to affect the attitudes and behavior of constituents. On no issue is this more evident than in the treatment that should be meted out to members of labor diasporas.

Dual loyalties

Beginning with the current era of the nation state, following the Westphalian settlement in Europe in 1648 of the bloody 30-year religious wars, through the spread of democracy and the extension of citizenship during the nineteenth century, the political allegiance of individuals was believed to be exclusive. A person could be a citizen of only a single nation state; should he or she accept naturalization in country B, it would first be necessary to renounce citizenship in country A. Citizenship could be achieved through either birth or naturalization. The suspicion of dual loyalty was a burden that some individuals who had shifted their allegiance tried hard to extirpate. Some Malays and Indonesians to this day suspect the loyalty of their locally born Chinese fellow citizens, even though Beijing has abandoned the policy of *ius sanguinis* and advised overseas Chinese to be loyal citizens of their country of residence. Prior to the election of President John F. Kennedy in 1960, Catholics in the US were suspected of primary loyalty to the Pope. When Muslim audiences in India cheered the victory of the Pakistan cricket squad over India's, many Indians charged their Muslim compatriots with primary loyalty to Pakistan, thus betraying their country of birth and residence.

Recently, as states have weakened in response to economic and informational globalization, as many as 90 states, including the United States, have relaxed their insistence on exclusive allegiance and begun to tolerate dual citizenship, on condition that the alternate citizenship is held in a country deemed to be not unfriendly to the US.[7] Israelis who have moved to the US and acquired American citizenship nevertheless retain their Israeli passports. The Mexican government has announced that Mexicans who migrate to the US and acquire American citizenship can continue to hold Mexican citizenship and vote in Mexican elections. Following the disintegration of the multinational Soviet Union and Yugoslavia, some US citizens accepted the invitation of successor regimes to occupy ministerial positions in their fledgling governments. In so doing, they were not required to renounce their American citizenship. Member states of the European Union, including Germany, that still adhere to the principle of exclusive nationality, might make it easier for members of their Turkish and other Middle Eastern and north African diasporas to accept citizenship in their countries if they were to permit concurrent dual citizenship.

For countries that acquiesce in dual citizenship, this has become a murky dimension of public policy. Can the second and successive generations continue to enjoy dual citizenship or does it apply only to original migrants? In which country, or in both, are they liable for taxation and military service? It seems reasonable to distinguish between countries that

adhere to exclusive citizenship and those that recognize concurrent citizenship in another country. Holders of dual
citizenship could be entitled to most of the rights and responsibilities of citizenship, including service in the armed forces,
but sacrifice some rights, such as the privilege of holding
office. While recognizing dual citizenship, this policy would
deny those who choose to share their political allegiance
some of the principal rights of traditional citizenship.

Policies toward religious minorities

What special rights should be conceded to diasporas that constitute religious minorities? In Christian-majority countries,
should kosher slaughter be allowed, in order to comply with
the dietary laws mandated for orthodox Jews, even though
animal rights activists insist that kosher slaughter inflicts unacceptable cruelty on its victims? Should Muslims be released
from work on Fridays to celebrate the Muslim Sabbath,
though this would disrupt production schedules and office
routines? Should Muslim women be permitted to wear headscarves in schools and government offices in violation of laws
and practices that prohibit the conspicuous display of sectar-
ian affiliation on government premises? In Muslim-majority
states, should members of Christian diasporas be permitted to
proselytize Muslims and Muslims be permitted to convert to
another faith? How far should religious freedom for minority
faiths and sects be privileged to override policies and customs
established by the majority? Or should diasporas, as minorities, be expected to adjust their religious practices to the rules
and customs of the national majority? Religious freedom, of
belief and of practice, is the bedrock, the most precious of
human rights. It should therefore be respected and privileged
in public policy – but only to the point that it threatens public
health, safety, or morals. Outlawing such religiously mandated practices as child marriage, honor killings, stoning for
adulterers, female genital mutilation – practices that offend
the emergent global consensus on human rights – would

constitute justifiable limitations by public policy on religious freedom.[8] But, does the wearing of headscarves by Muslim women threaten public safety, health, or morals?

Where membership is based on ethnicity

Countries where citizenship and membership in the political community are based on ethnicity or common descent have difficulty coping with cultural diversity. Members of diasporas, being ethnically foreign, can never qualify for admission to the national community, even though they have lived and worked in that country and their children are locally born, locally educated, fluent in the national language, and knowledgeable about local customs and lifestyles. Reluctant to recognize them formally as national minorities, governments keep them suspended in a status limbo. Japan's government, as we have observed, ignores their existence.

After decades of hesitation, Germany, where citizenship had been based on ethnic membership, has reformed its naturalization procedures in an effort to induce members of its longstanding Turkish diaspora to accept German citizenship.[9] Rather than face the prospect of a large, separatist minority in its midst, Germany's government finally agreed to revise its naturalization policy. Despite the misgivings of many rank-and-file Germans, its government now encourages a visibly "foreign" ethnic and religious diaspora to join their national political community with all the rights and privileges of German citizenship. The unacceptable alternative policy for Germany would have been de facto and eventual de jure recognition of its Turkish diaspora as a permanent minority with separate cultural institutions, such as schools, mosques, and mass media. The question that remains is how members of the Turkish diaspora will respond to this opportunity to join the German mainstream.

For countries that base their citizenship on adherence to a common civic culture and set of political institutions, the absorption of culturally diverse diasporas has been much less traumatic. Despite the resistance of nativist minorities, members of ethnic, racial, and religiously diverse communities are being admitted in large numbers to Canadian, Australian, and American citizenship. Once they accept the common language and political institutions of their adopted country, members of these diasporas are free, if they wish and as long as they wish, to cultivate localized versions of their inherited cultural institutions. This *inclusive policy* also allows diasporas, as they integrate to the national mainstream, to leave their mark on mainstream culture, solidifying thereby their sense of belonging to their adopted country.[10]

An inclusive policy facilitates integration if the target diaspora is inclined to accept integration – witness the Mexican diaspora in the United States, Russians in Israel, and Chinese in Thailand. It cannot induce integration for diasporas that insist on maintaining their separate collective identity, such as Hasidic Jews in the United States and Hindus in east Africa. Responses to *exclusionist policies* are less predictable. Some diasporas that have been marginalized continue, nevertheless, to hope for policy changes that will enable them to be accepted as equals: for example, Japanese-Americans prior to 1965 and Afro-Brazilians today. Others embittered by discrimination and rejection are likely to choose separation. Individuals in any diaspora may break away from the majority consensus. They may resist integration, while a majority of their community accepts it. They may opt for integration while a majority of their community refuses integration. Or they may construct hybrid identities that are part integrationist, part separatist. Thus, a minority of north African Muslims in France participate in mainstream educational and economic institutions, while retaining their affiliation with diaspora religious and cultural associations.

Mutable policies, mutable responses

We conclude this chapter on an optimistic note: *public policies are mutable, they are not engraved in stone.* Policies regarding diasporas can produce political disputes that culminate in revisions or reversals of earlier policies. External pressures, gradual shifts in domestic opinion, or political calculations precipitate policy changes both by governments and by diaspora communities. Canada, Australia, and the United States reversed their long-standing policies on Asian exclusion and began, in 1965, to admit large numbers of Asians on a non-discriminatory basis. Germany revised its naturalization procedures to encourage its hitherto reluctant Turkish diaspora to join Germany's mainstream community. It may not stretch credibility to expect that one day soon the government of Japan will recognize the reality of its chronic need for immigrant labor and begin to shape and implement policies to incorporate its diasporas into the national mainstream.

Responses of diasporas to government policies are similarly dynamic, reflecting changing circumstances and viewpoints. Prior to World War I, leading members of the large and proud German-American diaspora regarded German culture as superior to that of the American mainstream and aspired to establish a *Deutschtum*, a German-inspired civilization, in the United States. The shock of that war, in which Germany was America's enemy, convinced their constituents that there could be no German *Deutschtum* and that they must instead assert their American patriotism and participate in the English-language culture of their adopted country. Sino-Thai, who had earlier regarded themselves as Chinese nationals temporarily working overseas, took advantage of a more welcoming set of government policies to accommodate to Thai culture and accept Thai citizenship.

Generational succession provides the occasion for diasporas to rethink the central tendency of their collective strategy. For example, participation of a large number of second-generation Ukrainian-Canadians in the Canadian forces during World War II persuaded them to shift their collective strategy from a separatist to an integrationist orientation.

8
Prospects and outcomes

We have identified three classes of diasporas: labor, entrepreneurial, and settler. We have selected and analyzed
contemporary examples of each, chosen at random from
North and South America, Europe, Asia, and the Middle
East. Diasporas that belong to each of these classes have
certain properties that facilitate or constrain their adaptation to their new environment. What characterizes labor
diasporas is their sparse human and social capital, including
limited occupational and organizational skills. This exposes
them to exploitation, retards their occupational and social
mobility, and condemns them to slow access, both individu-
ally and collectively, to economic success and to positions of
influence and power in their host country. Entrepreneurial
diasporas, by contrast, capitalize on their business experience, educational backgrounds, and occupational skills to
gain economic and professional success and influence in their
adopted country, even in the face of unfriendly and resistant
opportunity structures. Where they encounter exclusion,
they innovate parallel economic and educational facilities to
handle their affairs. Settler diasporas, determined to assume
control over their adopted homeland, tend to overwhelm
their indigenous neighbors by superior military technology,
economic skills, and organizational capabilities.

Central tendencies and collective identities

The different trajectories that these diasporas experience result from the different capabilities of their members, their propensities to conform to the local mainstream, and the opportunity structures that they encounter. Like all human collectivities, diasporas are seldom monolithic; they include factions based on kinship attachments, economic interests, and ideological commitments. These factions compete to speak for the diaspora and to control its resources. Individuals may choose to go their own way, independently of these group attachments. In tracing the adaptation of diasporas to their new environment, we have attempted in every case to identify their central tendency, recognizing that some individuals or factions may depart from the group norm. Moreover, these central tendencies may shift over time, as members of the diaspora acquire additional capabilities, benefit from individual and organizational learning, or perceive changes in the opportunity structure that they encounter. Opportunity structures may likewise evolve, the result of external pressures or of internal political conflicts over the proper goals of their society.

Thus, the collective identities of diasporas are dynamic, as they adjust to new threats and fresh opportunities in their external environment. Their members may attempt simultaneously to share two ethnic identities, the inherited and the newly acquired, assuming a hybrid identity. With successive generations, the balance can shift, as the diaspora's culture adjusts to changing conditions. Individuals may reaffirm their inherited collective identity and endow it with fresh meaning; or they may abandon the diaspora altogether.

To cite a familiar example: Chinese in Thailand originally identified themselves as Chinese nationals working overseas. They espoused Chinese nationalism and contributed to the resistance against the Japanese invaders of their homeland. As Chinese nationalism and separatism encountered vigorous official hostility, while the opportunity structure invited them to abandon their Chinese identity and join the Thai political and cultural community, Sino-Thai, especially the second and third generation, agreed to conform by accepting Thai identity, learning and speaking the Thai language, adopting Thai surnames and the Theravada Buddhist faith, and joining the Thai mainstream. In many instances, they intermarried, retaining only vestigial elements of traditional Chinese culture. The shift in the collective identity of this diaspora over a few decades has been nearly complete. This contrasts with the experience of neighboring Chinese-Malaysians. Though formally citizens of their adopted country and economically successful, their social adaptation has been blocked by a rigidly unwelcoming opportunity structure. In the face of educational and economic discrimination and political marginalization, they retain their separate ethnic identity. As second-class Malaysians, they live apart from their Malay compatriots, compelled to build and rely on parallel political parties, educational facilities, religious institutions, and economic structures.

Citizenship in this case confers important rights and status, but not political or social equality; nor is it necessarily empowering. It does not ensure equal treatment in the government or private institutions of society. Like Palestinians in Israel, Chinese in Malaysia experience citizenship as a formal, but limited set of rights, while the ruling majority refuses to grant them equality of status or treatment, or access to the levers of political and social power.

Transnational enclaves

Initially, diasporas form residential enclaves that enable their members to reproduce their familiar environment. In these parallel societies they can enjoy the fellowship and protection of neighbors who share the same culture and speak the same language; they can participate in familiar religious, social, recreational, and educational activities. They maintain close contact with kinfolk and friends in the old country, renew these contacts by frequent communication and visits, and remit funds to aid their families. They follow athletic competitions, literary and theatrical productions, and political events back home, backing political causes that they favor with money, moral support, and sometimes personal participation. They may spend their entire lives in the shelter of their ethnic enclaves, physically and occupational in their host country, culturally and socially in the homeland they left behind.

They must, perforce, some more than others, begin to master the local language, interact with the political and especially the economic institutions of the mainstream, and adopt elements of the local lifestyle. But here the differences between labor and entrepreneurial diasporas become apparent. First-generation members of labor diasporas remain closely attached to their social enclave, while the more venturesome members of entrepreneurial diasporas seek out opportunities to participate in and benefit from the educational institutions of the mainstream, and to set up and operate their own businesses in economic niches that they discover. Some leave their diaspora enclave, take up residence in mainstream neighborhoods, and even intermarry. The more inclined they are to interact and the more open the opportunity structure, the easier their path of social mobility.

The break point is the second generation, locally educated, fluent in the mainstream language, at home with mainstream cultural and recreational idioms and lifestyles. Where the opportunity structure invites members of the second generation to look hopefully to their future, the transnational phase of their immigrant experience seldom extends beyond the first generation. Their interests and energies focus on making their way in their host country. But where their future seems blocked by a hostile and resistant opportunity structure, as with the north African Muslims of the second and subsequent generations in France and Spain, they nurse their grievances and frustrations by maintaining transnational linkages, often with dissident movements in the old country. Among labor diasporas, the second generation may remain in the enclave, even in the face of an open opportunity structure. Where the opportunity structure is resistant, they become embittered and hostile to the political establishment. When the second generation of an entrepreneurial diaspora encounters an open opportunity structure, its members move quickly into the business and professional ranks of the mainstream economy. Social assimilation is likely to follow. Where the local opportunity structure proves to be resistant, the children of entrepreneurial diasporas innovate their own social, cultural, and recreational associations, finding niches in the professions and the economy that enable them to prosper, even though their social mobility is hampered and they are forced to remain in their enclave outside the mainstream.

Opportunities and inclinations

The balance of frustrations and satisfactions conditions the posture of members of diasporas. The second and subsequent generations, locally born and educated, have expectations that differ from those of their immigrant forebears. If these expectations are gratified by a relatively open opportunity structure, integration into the mainstream will proceed apace, less rapidly and less smoothly for members of labor diasporas; more rapidly for their entrepreneurial counterparts. Those with no propensity to integrate, who value self-segregation, derive their satisfactions from being allowed to pursue their own way of life, like Amish in the United States. They find niches in the economy that enable them to earn their livelihoods and cope with the temptations that bid their youngsters to abandon the enclave and join the mainstream. Those, like north Africans in France, whose expectations are blocked, who experience discrimination or exclusion, may respond by matching rejection with rejection.

The integration of diasporas into the mainstream of their adopted country, their rejection or refusal, can be summarized by a simple matrix, drawing on cases analyzed in this

	Willing to be integrated	Unwilling to be integrated
Acceptable to mainstream	Sino-Thai Russians in Israel Mexicans in US Ukrainian Canadians	Amish in US
Unacceptable to mainstream	Afro-Brazilians Palestinians in Kuwait	North Africans in France Zionists in Palestine Sino-Malaysians

Figure 8.1   Inclinations and integration

text (see Figure 8.1). Those in the upper two rows enjoy a surplus of satisfactions; except for the Zionist settler diaspora, those in the bottom two quadrants suffer a net total of frustrations. These, once again, are central tendencies within the collectivity of their diasporas. In every case, outliers on the margins can attempt to alter their identities and leave the diaspora; or maintain tenuous links, while living, working, and raising their families outside its ranks.

Integration into the mainstream is a function of the local opportunity structure, modified by the propensity of the diaspora to integrate into the mainstream. Diasporas may endure for generations, even centuries, because, like Afro-Brazilians, they are excluded by the mainstream or, like Hasidic Jews, they insist on maintaining their separate identity and institutions. The pace of integration, and gradual dissolution of the diaspora – unless reinforced by fresh arrivals – depends on the capabilities of the diaspora: entrepreneurial diasporas, with their superior educational and occupational capabilities, are absorbed more rapidly than labor diasporas that are handicapped in these respects, Mexicans in the United States more slowly than Russians in Israel. Diasporas may be formed, flourish, and disappear in short order – Russians in Israel – as the second and subsequent generations adopt the local language and way of life, participate in mainstream economic and political institutions, intermarry, and depart the residential enclave.

Explaining the differences

In the Introduction, we asked what explains the differences in the reception of immigrant communities and in their responses. An answer emerges from the analysis in this book, from the different inclinations of individual diasporas and the different opportunity structures that confront them. The majority of recent immigrants in Europe, mostly Muslim, have been reluctant to join the mainstream in their host countries, fearing that this would constitute a betrayal of their inherited culture and religious traditions. Moreover, the opportunity structure in most European countries greeted them with an ambivalent, often hostile reception. Acceptable as needed laborers, they have been regarded as racially, religiously, and culturally unsuited for membership in the national community, and as security risks, potential terrorists, or terrorist sympathizers. Assamese natives in northeast India regard Bangladeshi immigrants with unalloyed suspicion as economic competitors and political threats. Hispanics and Asians in the United States, by contrast, have few cultural inhibitions against joining the mainstream and reaping the benefits of American citizenship. They encounter an opportunity structure that is experienced at absorbing immigrants. Despite nativist and lingering racist prejudice, they are permitted to participate in mainstream institutions and encouraged to qualify for citizenship.

At the University of Pittsburgh there are a series of "nationality rooms," each celebrating the culture of a diaspora that established itself in the Pittsburgh area at a time when Pittsburgh was the world center of heavy industry and jobs were plentiful.[1] Now in the third generation, the offsprings of these former immigrants have joined the American mainstream, participating fully in its institutions and in American popular culture, in many instances intermarrying. What remains of their ethnic cultures are snippets of their ancestral languages, culinary residues, and impressions of the old country and of the immigrant experience as related by their grandparents. They have responded to the opportunity structure that invited them to become fully

fledged Americans. Those with a distinctive religious identity, Greeks, Hindus, Jews, sustain a longer-term attachment
to their tradition, through a dual or hybrid identity, inherited and American. The nationality rooms remain as elegant
reminders of the cultures that their immigrant forebears left
behind, and of their contributions to their adopted country.
They have little relevance to the daily lives of the third and
subsequent American generations.

The contrary inclinations and expectations of immigrant
communities in Europe and America, combined with the
radically different opportunity structures they encounter –
these explain and account for the different experiences of
recent diasporas in Europe and the United States.

Ethnic conflict revisited

Diasporas of any size inevitably produce ethnic conflict. To
natives, these are foreigners, in some cases visibly different,
who speak strange languages, dress differently, eat strange
foods. They encroach on working-class neighborhoods, raising
the cost of rental housing. Labor diasporas are accused of
"stealing" jobs from native sons, lowering wage scales, violating labor standards, spreading diseases, committing crimes in
formerly peaceful neighborhoods. Entrepreneurial diasporas
are accused of operating businesses that employ sharp tactics,
drive local merchants to the wall, and exploit their customers. The local reaction mixes contempt with anger and fear,
fear that these "foreigners" threaten to change the character
of their neighborhoods, their cities, even their countries.
Politicians emerge, articulating these fears and insisting that
measures be taken by the authorities to limit further immigration, deport foreign law violators and illegal immigrants, and
curb the public expression of diaspora languages. Employers
who value the hard-working, uncomplaining immigrant
workers may defend them from more serious efforts at discrimination; they are joined in coalitions by religious, civil
libertarian, and human rights organizations. Immigrants may

be tolerated as long as they stay in their own part of town, remain invisible, perform jobs that natives avoid, and do not cause trouble, being accused at the same time of clannishness and refusal to mix with local people.

As conflicts become politicized, native sons demand new laws and administrative measures to limit the rights of immigrants to public services, and to enforce existing laws against criminal acts of which they are accused. The diaspora and its sympathizers organize to resist these threats, search for allies, and place their own demands on the political agenda. These charges and countercharges evoke controversy, yet they can be managed civilly and compromised within the rules of the political system. They may, however, break out into violence – violence provoked by the frustrations of the second generation of the diaspora, compounded by police harassment or by indigenous hostility to perceived encroachments by foreigners. The violence may be limited to areas populated by immigrants, as with the north African uprising in French suburbs in October 2005; or consist of sporadic attacks against government targets anywhere in the country, such as the suicide bombing by Islamist terrorists of a commuter train in 2004, which killed 191 people in Madrid. Or it may break out into insurrection that seeks control of the state, as with the Chinese-led rebellion in Malaya from 1948 to 1960. Demonstrating the likelihood of divisions in every diaspora, a substantial faction of Malayan-Chinese opposed that insurrection. They condemned it as a communist conspiracy, cooperated with the British, and joined the Malay-led Alliance Party that formed the government of independent Malaya.

Spain is host to more than a million north Africans who have made the short crossing from Morocco in search of work. They now provide the essential labor force in the important construction and agricultural industries. But Spain's local governments have been unwilling to allow members of this diaspora to build proper mosques in their communities.[2] Such disrespect for their religion exacerbates relations between government and this diaspora community.

Once an immigrant community has been allowed to establish itself within a country, they may be confronted with disrespect, discrimination, and exclusion (for example, no mosques or no headscarves), leading to disaffection; or their culture may be treated with respect and its members encouraged to participate in the institutions of the mainstream. Hostility to Muslims in Spain may be traced to recent instances of terrorist violence, coupled with Spaniards' collective memory of the seven centuries of Muslim rule in large areas of their country which ended in 1492; and fear that this diaspora is but the first wave of an avenging campaign to reestablish Islamic rule in Al Andulus.

Transnational population movements

By the midpoint of the present century, world population will exceed 9 billion, of whom three-quarters will reside in low-income, labor-surplus countries.[3] There will be powerful incentives for many to move, legally or illegally, to countries that offer them opportunities for a better way of life. The transnational flow of immigrants diminishes and may even reverse during periods of economic recession in the wealthy countries when jobs become scarce, as during the American recession of 2008–9. Remittances of funds from diasporas to families back home stagnate and even decline. But, as these economies recover and their demand for labor is renewed, immigration resumes and diasporas are renewed with fresh recruits.

As long as wage rates and living standards remain significantly higher in some countries than in others; as long as men and women feel oppressed or excluded from opportunities due to membership in religious, ethnic, or political minorities; as long as warfare and other forms of organized violence produce refugees, people will move in substantial numbers across international borders, seeking greater security or opportunities for themselves and their families. They will form diaspora communities similar to those analyzed in chapter 3.

While European governments, in response to public

opinion, close their doors to further immigration (except from member countries of the European Union), the United Nations Population Division projects that European economies will need a million new immigrants annually during the next half-century to maintain their present population and meet the demand for labor. As long as the demand exists, it will be supplied by immigrants, legal or illegal. Most will be visible, culturally exotic Muslims, disinclined to become European and in any case unacceptable to most Europeans as fellow citizens. Some diasporas, as in Japan, must exist *sub rosa*, since Japan's authorities cling to the myth of the pure Yamato race which must avoid contamination by foreigners. Meantime, Japan's declining population is unable to provide the labor needed to operate its economy.

The fate of the Palestinian community in Kuwait is an example of the precarious status of foreign workers in many host countries, including the petroleum economies of the Persian Gulf states. They are recruited, often by labor contractors, with the clear stipulation that they will return to their native countries at the conclusion of their contracts unless these are formally renewed. Contract workers outnumber local residents. They perform many of the professional, managerial, skilled and unskilled labor functions necessary to operate the economy and the public services. They are highly compensated by the standards of their home countries, sufficient in many cases to build houses or establish new businesses when they return home. Barred from aspiring to citizenship or even permanent residence, they may not acquire property and they have no access to indigenous women. They are rigidly excluded from local society. In fact, the Gulf States have learned to prefer Asian non-Muslims – Indians, Sri Lankans, Filipinos – since these contract guest workers can claim no special rights as brother Arabs or Muslims. Like the Palestinians, they can be summarily deported if suspected of hostility or subversion. While performing their contracts, these guest workers form diaspora communities to provide for their religious, social, recreational, and entertainment needs and the schooling of their children.

Diaspora prospects and outcomes

We have identified both intermediate prospects and longer-term outcomes for diasporas.

Intermediate prospects

Polarization and mutual intermingling are intermediate prospects that are illustrated by examples from our analysis.

The north African diaspora in France is a good example of *ethnic polarization*. Despite a large measure of acculturation, by the second generation, their central tendency has been shaped by high levels of unemployment, occupational discrimination, perceived disrespect for their religion and culture, and rejection by the French mainstream. This has resulted in attitudinal alienation from French society and its institutions, and violent behavior by its youth. Polarization of this intensity is a certain indicator of impending conflict, with the likelihood of violence. A lesser degree of polarization is evident among Malaysian Chinese, who remain, after several generations, a culturally and socially separate community, but whose economic success has blunted the pain of social exclusion and second-class citizenship. It has directed their grievances into peaceful political channels and in some instances into emigration. By discrimination and social exclusion, the White Brazilian mainstream refuses to integrate the descendants of its former slave population as people of color, in defiance of the prevailing myth that Brazil is a color-blind society and of laws that criminalizes racial discrimination. Afro-Brazilians continue to plead for equal incorporation and the end of polarization. Palestinians in Syria and Lebanon are held at arm's length from these societies by exclusionist opportunity structures. Consequently, they remain psychologically exiles, yearning not to become Syrians or Lebanese, but to return to their former homeland.

Despite lingering prejudice and lagging progress among its high school dropouts, the beginnings of *mutual intermingling* are evident among Mexican-Americans in the United States.

Many members of the second and subsequent generations of this diaspora, having acculturated to the American mainstream, live in mixed neighborhoods, intermarry, and participate in the religious, educational, economic, and political institutions of mainstream America.[4] Having added tacos to the ethnic fare of pizza and bagels, and *hasta la vista* to colloquial banter, the mainstream has signaled its willingness to encourage acculturation and assimilate members of its Mexican-American diaspora who are in the country legally. Undocumented (illegal) Mexican immigrants remain an issue of domestic political controversy between nativists who would punish and deport them as law-breakers, and those who would enable them, after living and working in the United States for several years and paying a substantial fine, to achieve legal status and qualify eventually for citizenship.

Considerable intermingling is also evident between members of the Sino-Thai diaspora in Thailand and that society, and, on a lesser scale, between Russians in Israel and mainstream Israelis.

Longer-term prospects

What of the longer-term fate of diasporas? We have identified four longer-term outcomes. They disappear, they become the mainstream, they integrate into the mainstream, or they survive as subordinated minorities.

Diasporas *disappear* if 1) they are expelled like Palestinians from Kuwait or Asians from Uganda in the 1960s, or 2) they are completely absorbed by the mainstream and lose their identity, like Dutch and Czechs in the United States and Poles in France.

Becoming the mainstream has become the goal of settler diasporas, soon realized in our example by Zionists in Palestine. Settler diasporas expel or subordinate the previous inhabitants, assume control, and become the mainstream in the territories they have conquered and settled. By similar measures, British Protestant settlers became the mainstream in North America.

They are *integrated* gradually into the national mainstream by virtue of their own inclination combined with a welcoming opportunity structure. Sino-Thai, Mexican-American, Russian-Israeli, and Ukrainian-Canadian diaspora communities are well on their way in the evolution from mutual intermingling to successful integration into the mainstream of their adopted homelands. In none of these cases is the progress from mutual intermingling to integration likely to be blocked, delayed, or reversed.

Members of diaspora communities whose cohesion is reinforced by a distinctive religious tradition tend to maintain this connection and cultivate a hybrid identity, while integrating into the culture and lifestyles of the mainstream. This applies to Armenian, Greek, and Jewish diasporas in the United States, which are joining the mainstream, while continuing to participate in their inherited religious institutions.

Many of the diasporas that have experienced polarization become *subordinated minorities*. Frustrated and embittered by the constraints of a hostile and unyielding opportunity structure, they nevertheless remain in their host country because of inertia or because they are unaware of alternative sites where they would be better treated. The majority of Muslim diasporas in Europe find themselves rejected by their European hosts, reinforcing their disinclination to become Europeans, fearing that this would betray their inherited culture. Though marginalized socially and politically, entrepreneurial "middleman" diasporas, like Malaysian-Chinese, may achieve higher living standards than members of the indigenous majority that rejects them socially and politically. Some subordinated diasporas may be tolerated and allowed a significant measure of self-determination, as long as their members remain quiescent and cause no problems for the mainstream – for example, Christians and Jews in the former Ottoman Empire. They may, however, with little warning, be targeted as scapegoats for the frustrations of majority communities and suffer severe damage to lives and property, like Chinese in Indonesia during the 1990s.

What can be done?

What can governments do to foster integration and minimize the risk of disruptive ethnic conflict, resulting from immigration and the formation of ethnic diasporas? The answer is evident from the cases analyzed in this study.

Except for those who arrive under specific, time-bound contract arrangements, the local opportunity structure should enable immigrants who are legally admitted for their labor or occupational skills, especially their locally born progeny, to gain educational credentials, participate in the economy on a non-discriminatory basis, and aspire to citizenship; in short, to gain a sense of valuing and belonging to their host country. By their example and by their policies, governments should encourage their citizenry to accept the new arrivals and their locally born offsprings, despite cultural differences and distinctive appearances, as potential recruits to the national political community. They should be willing to accept unthreatening expressions of cultural diversity as elements of a policy to secure their allegiance by accommodating small differences. France should allow Muslim students to wear headscarves in school, and Spanish local authorities should permit the construction of proper mosques.

Whether their members, once they have moved out of diaspora residential enclaves and into mainstream neighborhoods, choose to blend into mainstream society, prefer to remain socially apart, or adopt a dual, hybrid identity, retaining with co-ethnics some elements of their ancestral culture, they would have few grievances to cultivate. The national goal should be to incorporate members of resident diasporas into the mainstream. But members of minority immigrant communities who resist incorporation into the mainstream and prefer to remain a community apart should be recognized and respected as a minority, and allowed to maintain their culture, as long as they abide peacefully by the country's laws.

Immigrants move across international borders and are admitted, usually for economic reasons. Their labor is needed or their skills are believed to contribute to economic development. Only after they have settled and been joined by family members do questions of their suitability and acceptability for membership in the national community begin to arise. Conflict emerges when it becomes clear to members of the second and third generations of the diaspora that their presence has evoked hostility or militant opposition among elements of the indigenous society, that the local opportunity structure excludes them from equal access to and participation in its educational and economic institutions, that their occupational and social mobility is blocked by discrimination and marginalization, that their culture and religion are disrespected, and that they cannot aspire to treatment as social or political equals.

Diasporas that are disaffected by mainstream rejection no longer expect to join local society; nor do they intend to leave the country. Hostility and rejection notwithstanding, they are in the country to stay. They may manifest their disaffection by sullen compliance or by sporadic outbreaks of violence. Factions among them may opt for recognition as a separate society with minority cultural and political rights, a status that is likely to be problematic for members of the native majority. Some, like Afro-Brazilians, will continue to plead for changes in mainstream attitudes and public policy that will open the opportunity structure to them on a non-discriminatory basis. Few countries are prepared to implement the draconian measure of mass expulsion of a community whose labor or enterprise is still required. They are thus confronted with the permanent presence in their midst of a disaffected diaspora. Some may break away from the majority consensus and, as individuals, seek ways through education or economic innovation to participate in mainstream institutions, overcoming the prevailing discrimination. A few join terrorist cells, bent on violent reactions against what they regard as an oppressive government and society.

A relatively open opportunity structure that is prepared to tolerate, if not to welcome, ethnic diversity is most likely to foster integration and minimize the prospect of violent conflict. If, on the other hand, the national preference is to retain ethnic purity, real or imagined, then immigration should be forbidden or rigidly controlled to admit only those of suitable ethnic provenance; or permitted only for contract labor under close supervision and with strictly enforced time limits. If the economy requires outsiders, they will manage to trickle in, evading local enforcement, concealed and often exploited by employers, living a clandestine existence. Sooner or later barriers to permanent residence will erode; government and its society will then be confronted with unwanted diasporas.

When immigration becomes necessary for whatever reason, humane or economic, an open, inclusive opportunity structure for those who are admitted is the most sensible approach to minimizing the long-term prospect of a disaffected domestic minority. Lingering nativist aspirations for a fictitious ethnic purity must be compelled to yield to economic necessity and, consequently, to the inevitability of ethnic diversity. Meantime, incentives should be provided for members of diasporas to acculturate and participate in mainstream institutions as stepping-stones to political and social integration.

Notes

INTRODUCTION

1   Philip Johnston, "The Shadow Cast by the Mega Mosque," *Daily Telegraph*, September 25, 2006; "London Mosque Scaled Down, No Longer the Largest in Europe," *Network Europe*, January 25, 2008.

CHAPTER 1   WHAT ARE DIASPORAS, WHY DO THEY MATTER?

1   Genesis 46.9, Exodus 1.14.
2   Population and Social Integration Section, UN Economic and Social Council, November 27, 2006.
3   Dilip Ratha et al., *Migration and Development Brief 5*, Washington: World Bank, July 10, 2008.
4   Reported in *The Economist*, January 20, 2007, p. 54.
5   For a brief review of the constructionist approach to ethnicity, see Milton J. Esman, *An Introduction to Ethnic Conflict*, Cambridge, UK: Polity, 2004, pp. 34–5. For a more extended treatment, see Benedict Anderson, *Imagined Communities: Reflections on the Origin and Spread of Nationalism*, London: Verso, 1991.
6   Hugh Muir and Riazat Butt, "A Rumour, Outrage, and Then a Riot: How Tensions in a Birmingham Suburb Erupted," *Guardian*, October 24, 2005.

CHAPTER 2 DEFINITION AND CLASSES OF DIASPORAS

1 Robin Cohen, *Global Diasporas: An Introduction*, Seattle, WA: University of Washington Press, 1997, p. 26.
2 This is contrary to William Safran's influential article, "Diasporas in Modern Societies: Myths of Homeland and Return," *Diaspora* 1(1), pp. 83–91, in which his several properties of diasporas emphasize the continuing commitment to their original homeland, including their aspiration to eventually return.
3 Jana Evans Braziel and Anita Mannur (eds.), *Theorizing Diasporas: A Reader*, Oxford: Blackwell, 2003, is an edited collection of previously published articles from the constructionist perspective by anthropologists and literary specialists. Each chapter concludes with an extended bibliography. The introductory chapter by the editors may be of special interest. It speculates on the concept, scope, and dimensions of diasporas in the context of contemporary capitalist globalization.
4 Lawrence J. McCaffrey, *The Irish Diaspora in America*, Bloomington, IN: Indiana University Press, 1976; Gabriel Sheffer (ed.), *Modern Diasporas in International Politics*, London: Croom Helm, 1986; Nicholas Van Hear, *New Diasporas: The Mass Exodus, Dispersal and Regrouping of Migrant Communities*, Seattle, WA: University of Washington Press, 1998; Jana Evans Braziel and Anita Mannur (eds.), *Theorizing Diasporas: A Reader*, Oxford: Blackwell, 2003; Rainer Munz and Rainer Ohliger (eds.), *Diasporas and Ethnic Migrants: Germany, Israel, and Post-Soviet Successor States in Comparative Perspective*, London: Frank Cass, 2003; The Routledge-Washington series on global diasporas, including Vic Satzewich, *The Ukrainian Diaspora*, New York: Routledge, 2002; Darshan Singh Tatla, *The Sikh Diaspora: The Search for Statehood*, Seattle, WA: University of Washington Press, 1999; Donna R. Gabaccia, *Italy's Many Diasporas*, London: UCL Press, 2000; Steven Vertovec, *The Hindu Diaspora, Comparative Patterns*, New York: Routledge, 2000; Steven J. Gold, *The Israeli Diaspora*, Seattle, WA: University of Washington Press, 2002.
5 Imperial powers that gain control of a foreign territory and its people in order to spread their religion and culture, exploit the territory's resources, or implement a strategic objective, but

without fostering foreign settlement, have not created settler diasporas. Americans in the Philippines, British in India, French in Indo-China, and Japanese in Manchuria are examples of conquest and domination without substantial settlements.

6 Edna Bonacich, "A Theory of Middleman Minorities," *American Sociological Review*, 1973, pp. 583–94.

7 Jennifer Brinkerhoff, *Digital Diasporas: Identity and Transnational Engagement*, New York: Cambridge University Press, forthcoming.

8 See Stephen Cornell and Douglas Hartman, *Ethnicity and Race: Making Identities in a Changing World*, Thousand Oaks, CA: Pine Forge Press, 1998.

CHAPTER 3 CONTEMPORARY CASE STUDIES

1 Reported by Geraldine Baum in the *Los Angeles Times*, February 9, 2008.

2 On the meaning of the terms and the distinctions between *ius sanguinis* and *ius soli*, see Diane Orentlicher, "Citizenship and National Identity" in David Wippman (ed.), *International Law and Ethnic Conflict*, Ithaca, NY: Cornell University Press, 1998, pp. 317–19.

3 Victor Purcell, *The Chinese in Southeast Asia*, Oxford: Oxford University Press, 1965. Also Wang Gungwu, *The Chinese Overseas*, Cambridge, MA: Harvard University Press, 2000.

4 J. S. Furnival first developed the concept of plural societies for southeast Asia. *Colonial Policy and Practice: A Comparative Study of Burma and Netherlands India*, Cambridge: Cambridge University Press, 1948.

5 Overseas Chinese Affairs Commission, *Overseas Chinese Economy Yearbook*, Taipeh, 1999.

6 The concept of middleman minorities was developed by Edna Bonacich and John Modell in their *Economic Basis of Ethnic Solidarity: A Study of Japanese-Americans*, Berkeley, CA: University of California Press, 1980.

7 Karl Von Vorys, *Democracy Without Consensus: Communalism and Political Stability in Malaysia*, Princeton, NJ: Princeton University Press, 1975.

8 In the February 2008 election, the National Front retained its control of Parliament, but with a reduced majority, less

than the customary two-thirds that enabled it to amend the Constitution. It also lost control of five state governments.

9   Harold Crouch, *Government and Society in Malaysia*, Ithaca, NY: Cornell University Press, 1995. Also Milton J. Esman, *Administration and Development in Malaysia*, Ithaca, NY: Cornell University Press, 1974; Edmund T. Gomez and K. S. Jomo, *Malaysia's Political Economy: Politics, Patronage, and Profits*, Cambridge: Cambridge University Press, 1997.

10 "Putting the *Malaise* into Malaysia," *The Economist*, December 2, 2006, pp. 45–46.

11 Malaysians of Indian origin, mostly Tamil and Sikh, about 9 percent of the population, have participated in the National Front through the Malaysian Indian Congress. They nevertheless complain about discrimination and marginalization. Recently they have protested about threats to their religious freedom resulting from the destruction of several Hindu houses of worship; and a *cause célèbre* when a soldier of Indian origin who had died was claimed for burial by Muslim authorities as a recent convert to Islam, which his Hindu family vigorously denied. Thomas Fuller, "Indians' Discontent Fuels Malaysia's Rising Tensions," *New York Times*, February 10, 2008, p. A6.

12 World Bank, *Migration and Remittances Factbook*, Washington DC, March 2008.

13 Walter F. Vella, *Chaiyo! King Vajiravudh and the Development of Thai Nationalism*, Honolulu: East-West Center Press, 1995.

14 Supong Chantavanich, "From Siamese-Chinese to Chinese-Thai: Political Conditions and Identity Shifts Among Chinese in Thailand," in Leo Suryadinata (ed.), *Ethnic Chinese as Southeast Asians*, Singapore: Institute of Southeast Asian Studies, 1997, chapter 7, pp. 232–59.

15 Michael Vatikiotis, "Thailand, Sino-Chic: Suddenly it's Cool to be Chinese," *Far Eastern Economic Review*, January 11, 1996, p. 22.

16 Estimates by Tabito Arudou, "Japan's Future as an International Multicultural Society: From Migrants to Immigrants," *Japan Focus: An Asia-Pacific e-Journal*, October 29, 2007. Sakanaka Hidenori, former director of the Immigration Bureau in the Ministry of Justice, estimated the need at 400,000 annually (20 million during the next 50 years). "The Future of Japan's Immigration Policy," *Japan Focus*, April 15, 2007, translated by Andrew Taylor and David McNeill.

17 Daojiong Zha, "Chinese Migrant Workers in Japan: Policies, Institutions, and Civil Society," Monterey Institute of International Studies, 2003.

18 Alfred Dreyfus, a Jewish officer in the French army, was accused of passing French military secrets to Germany. He was convicted in a court-martial, disgraced, and imprisoned on Devil's Island. The "Dreyfus affair" became a hot political issue in France. An intense campaign by his family and sympathizers culminated in the celebrated pamphlet by Emile Zola, *J'accuse*, in which he charged members of the army's high command with railroading an innocent man to prison based entirely on crude anti-Semitism. After five years in prison, Dreyfus was vindicated, his army commission was restored in a public ceremony, and his oppressors were dismissed from the army in disgrace. This strain of reactionary anti-Semitism resurfaced four decades later in the Vichy regime that collaborated with the Nazis during the German occupation of France. There is an extensive literature on the Dreyfus affair in French. In English, see Michael Burns, *France and the Dreyfus Affair: A Documentary History*, Boston: Bedford/St Martin's, 1999.

19 On the history of modern Zionism, the most detailed account is the magisterial three-volume work by David Vital, published by the Clarendon Press at Oxford (see Bibliography). For a more concise account, see Mordecai S. Chertoff, *Zionism: A Basic Reader*, New York: Herzl Press, 1975.

20 On the circumstances surrounding the Balfour Declaration, see Ronald Sanders, *The High Walls of Jerusalem: A History of the Balfour Declaration*, New York: Holt, Rinehart, and Winston, 1984.

21 On relations between Israelis and Palestinians, there are large bodies of polemical publications on both sides. For a balanced treatment, see Fred Khouri, *The Arab–Israel Dilemma*, Syracuse, New York: Syracuse University Press, 3rd edition, 1985.

22 On Palestinian nationalism and the PLO, see Diane L. Reische, *Arafat and the Palestine Liberation Organization*, New York: F. Watts, 1991.

23 On the Camp David Accords that resulted in the Israeli peace treaty with Egypt, its largest neighbor, see Shibley Telhami, *Power and Leadership in International Bargaining: The Path to the Camp David Accords*, New York: Columbia University

Press, 1990.

24 On the Oslo Accords, see Gilead Sher, *The Israeli–Palestinian Peace Negotiations, 1999–2001: Within Reach*, London and New York: Routledge, 2006.

25 Reported by Eetta Prince-Gibson in the *Jerusalem Report*, November 26, 2007, pp. 13–15.

26 Estimated by Ann Lancyk, *Ukraine and Ukrainians Throughout the World*, Toronto: University of Toronto Press, 1994.

27 Vic Satzewich, *The Ukrainian Diaspora*, London and New York: Routledge, 2002, p. 10.

28 Orest Subtelny, *Ukraine: A History*, Toronto: University of Toronto Press, 1994, p. 480, cited by Satzewich, *The Ukrainian Diaspora*, p. 86.

29 Satzewich, *The Ukrainian Diaspora*, p. 17.

30 The Royal Commission's report, issued in 1969, led to the Official Languages Act of 1969, which established French and English, the languages of Canada's two "founding races," as the official languages of the government of Canada.

31 For a detailed analysis of this confrontation, see Harold Troper and Morton Weinfeld, *Old Wounds: Jews, Ukrainians and the Hunt for Nazi War Criminals in Canada*, Markham, Ontario: Penguin, 1988.

32 This theme is analyzed in depth by Satzewich, *The Ukrainian Diaspora*, chapter 8, pp. 190–213.

33 The debates among Ukrainian-Canadians about prospects for the survival of their diasporas in North America are evaluated by Satzewich, *The Ukrainian Diaspora*, pp. 221–2.

34 The Helsinki Accords of August 1975 committed the Soviet Union to respect a broad range of human rights, including the right to emigrate, in return for recognition by the US and its NATO allies of Soviet territorial gains from World War II in eastern Europe.

35 Majid Al-Haj, *Immigration and Ethnic Formation in a Deeply Divided Society: The Case of the 1990s Immigration from the Former Soviet Union*, Leiden, Netherlands: Brill, 2004, pp. 102–15.

36 Allan S. Galper, *From Bolshoi to Be'er Sheva, Scientists to Street Sweepers*, Lanham, MD, University Press of America, 1995. This is the not uncommon experience of high-status immigrants encountering a society whose language, customs, and methods of working are unfamiliar to them.

37 Tamar Horowitz, "Integration or Separatism," in Tamar Horowitz (ed.), *Children of Perestroika in Israel*, Lanham, MD: University Press of America, 1999, pp. 1–21.

38 Zinaida Ilatov and Shmuel Shamai, "Segmented Absorption: Israeli Students' View of Soviet Immigrant Students," in Horowitz (ed.), *Children of Perestroika in Israel*, pp. 205–17.

39 Al-Haj, *Immigration and Ethnic Formation*, p. 154.

40 Al-Haj, *Immigration and Ethnic Formation*, pp. 154–6.

41 Al-Haj, *Immigration and Ethnic Formation*, pp. 178–80, 205–20.

42 Not all communities of former slaves in the Americas can be considered diasporas in the twenty-first century. Afro-Caribbeans have become mainstream in the several Caribbean nations. Since the Civil Rights revolution in the United States in the 1960s, despite lingering prejudice and racist sentiment, increasing numbers of African-Americans have been moving into the mainstream as academics, corporate executives, and public officials, including the newly elected President Obama.

43 As a result, "miscegenation has long been a defining metaphor of the Brazilian nation." Edward E. Telles, *Race in Another America: The Significance of Skin Color in Brazil*, Princeton, NJ: Princeton University Press, 2004, p. 4. On whitening, see Abdias do Nascimento and Elisa Larkin Nascimento, "Dance of Deception: A Reading of Race Relations in Brazil," in Charles V. Hamilton et al. (eds.), *Beyond Racism: Race and Inequality in Brazil, South Africa and the United States*, Boulder, CO: Lynne Rienner, 2001, pp. 122–5.

44 Antonio Sergio Alfredo Guimaraes, "The Misadventures of Non-racialism: Race and Inequality in Brazil," in Hamilton et al. (eds.), *Beyond Racism*, pp. 157–86.

45 Rebecca Reichmann (ed.), *Race in Contemporary Brazil*, University Park, PA: Penn State University Press, 1999, p. 8.

46 Data reported by Edna Maria Santos Roland, "The Economics of Racism: People of African Descent in Brazil," paper presented at the Seminar on the Economics of Racism, Geneva, sponsored by the International Council on Human Rights Policy, November 24–5, 2001. These data are summarized by Darien J. Davis, *Afro-Brazilians: Time for Recognition*, London: Minority Rights Group International, 1999, p. 32.

47 Abdias do Nascimento and Elisa Larkin Nascimento, "Dance of Deception: A Reading of Race Relations in Brazil," in

Hamilton et al. (eds.), *Beyond Racism*, pp. 157–86.

48 Larry Rohter, "Soccer Skirmish Turns Spotlight on Brazil's Racial Divide," *New York Times*, September 19, 2006, p. A4.

49 Davis, *Afro-Brazilians*, pp. 25–6.

50 Telles, *Race in Another America*, p. 220.

51 Davis, *Afro-Brazilians*, pp. 27–9.

52 Joao Jose Reis, *Slave Rebellions in Brazil: The Muslim Uprising in 1835 in Bahia* (trans. Arthur Brakel), Baltimore, MD: Johns Hopkins University Press, 1993.

53 On Blacks in politics, see Davis, *Afro-Brazilians*, pp. 22–3.

54 Nascimento and Nascimento, "Dance of Deception," pp. 128–30.

55 Data from the Gaetulio Vargas Foundation, reported in *The Economist*, April 14, 2007, p. 12.

56 Elisa Larkin Nascimento, "It's in the Blood: Notes on Race Attitudes in Brazil from a Different Perspective," in Hamilton et al. (eds.), *Beyond Racism*, pp. 509–25.

57 The persistence of Afro-Brazilian cultural themes and practices, particularly in the northeast is elaborated in the edited volume by Hendrik Kraay, *Afro-Brazilian Culture and Politics, Bahia, 1790 to 1990*, Armonk, NY: M. E. Sharpe, 1998.

58 Prior to the oil boom, Kuwait's traditional economy was dominated by pearl divers and merchants, who exchanged the products of the Bedouin desert economy for imported merchandise.

59 Yet Longva found individuals among the second generation, born and raised in Kuwait, who regarded Kuwait as their homeland, despite their legal status as aliens. Anh Nga Longva, *Walls Built on Sand: Migration, Exclusion, and Society in Kuwait*, Boulder CO: Westview Press, 1997, pp. 78–9.

60 The psychology of temporariness is analyzed by Longva, *Walls Built on Sand*, pp. 177–84.

61 Longva, *Walls Built on Sand*, p. 48.

62 The institution of *kafala* regulated the status of non-Kuwaiti workers. The Kuwaiti citizen sponsors and assumes responsibility for immigrants who work for him or her. Longva, *Walls Built on Sand*, pp. 78–9.

63 Longva, *Walls Built on Sand*, p. 229.

64 Onn Winckler, *Demographic Developments and Population Policies in Kuwait*, Tel Aviv: Moshe Dayan Center for Middle East and African Studies, 1998, pp. 23–4.

65 To enhance their precarious sense of security, some of the more affluent Palestinians acquired apartments or houses in Europe, mainly in England. Longva, *Walls Built on Sand*, p. 159.

66 For a detailed Palestinian perspective on the expulsion and ethnic cleansing of Palestinians from Kuwait, see Hassan A. El Najjar, *The Gulf War: Overreaction and Excessiveness*, Dalton, GA: Amazone Press, 2001, chapter X, "Palestinians in Kuwait."

67 During the Great Depression the number of Mexican immigrants in the US was reduced by half. Oscar J. Martinez, *Mexican Origin People in the US*, Tucson, AZ: University of Arizona Press, 2001, p. 13.

68 As many as 3.5 million Mexican workers participated in the Bracero program. Martinez, *Mexican Origin People in the US*, p. 33.

69 Some 37 million persons in the United States in the year 2000 were foreign-born. A majority of the fast-growing illegal immigrant population is from Mexico. During the 1990s, an annual average of one million Mexicans seeking to enter the United States illegally were apprehended and sent back to Mexico. This did little to stem the flow of undocumented Mexican immigrants, however, as those who fail the first time keep trying until they finally succeed. Several hundred die annually of exhaustion and thirst, seeking to cross the Arizona desert on foot.

70 That number declined by an estimated 50 percent during the economic recession of 2007–8, as employment opportunities decreased markedly, especially in the construction industry.

71 The Pew Hispanic Center reports that naturalization among Mexican-Americans is increasing rapidly, though Mexicans remain less likely than other immigrants to become citizens. *New York Times*, March 29, 2007, p. A18.

72 This referendum was approved by California voters, but declared unconstitutional by the courts.

73 La Raza works through more than 220 community-based organizations. Pastora San Juan Cafferty and David W. Egstrom (eds.), *Hispanics in the United States*, New Brunswick, NJ: Transaction, 2000, p. 335.

74 Some 90 percent of Mexican-Americans are in low-skill occupations. Cafferty and Egstrom (eds.), *Hispanics in the United States*, p. 185.

75 The poverty rate for Mexican-Americans is double the national average. Martinez, *Mexican Origin People in the US*, p. 127.

76 The Inter-American Development Bank estimates remittances from Mexican-Americans to Mexico totaled $20 billion in 2005, exceeded only by tourism as a foreign exchange earner for Mexico's economy.

77 Frank D. Bean, Rodolfo O. de la Garza, Bryan R. Roberts and Sidney Weintraub, *At the Crossroads: Mexican Migration and US Policy*, Lanham, MD: Rowman and Littlefield, 1997, p. 131.

78 Christine Marie Sierra, "Hispanics and the Political Process," in Cafferty and Egstrom (eds.), *Hispanics in the United States*, p. 331.

79 Data from Latino Policy Coalition Survey, September 2006, reported in David L. Leal, Stephen A. Nuno, Jongho Lee, and Rodolfo de la Garza, "Latinos, Immigration, and the 2006 Midterm Elections," *PS: Political Science and Politics*, 41(2), pp. 309–18. The authors argue that Latinos cannot be considered a swing voting bloc because they predictably vote Democratic.

80 These different experiences are detailed throughout the volume edited by Victor Zuniga and Ruben Hernandez-Leon, *New Destinations: Mexican Immigration in the United States*, New York: Russell Sage Foundation, 2005.

81 Military service by Mexican-Americans is discussed by Martinez, *Mexican Origin People in the US*, pp. 82–7.

82 Data reported by the Los Angeles Police Department, cited in *The Economist*, August 4, 2007, p. 26.

83 On racism directed at Mexican-Americans, see Martinez, *Mexican Origin People in the US*, pp. 51–72.

84 Fear that recent Hispanic immigration, including Mexican, is overwhelming the nation's absorptive capacity and may constitute a parallel Spanish-speaking, Hispanic culture within the borders of the United States is not confined to uneducated rednecks and super-patriots. Many of these same fears were expressed by the Harvard political scientist, Samuel P. Huntington, in his recent book, *Who Are We? The Challenge to America's Identity*, New York: Simon and Schuster, 2004.

85 Zuniga and Hernandez-Leon (eds.), *New Destinations*, p. 189.

86 Edward E. Telles and Vilma Ortiz, *Generations of Exclusion: Mexican-Americans, Assimilation and Race*, New York: Russell Sage Foundation, 2008, p. 265.

87   On the small but growing cohort of the Mexican-American
     middle class, see Martinez, *Mexican Origin People in the US*,
     pp. 191–2.
88   In 1995, Mexico's government authorized dual citizenship.
     This enables Mexican-American citizens of the US to vote in
     Mexican elections. Martinez, *Mexican Origin People in the US*,
     pp. 198–9.

CHAPTER 4 PROBLEMS AND PROCESSES OF ADAPTATION

1   Jennifer Jackson-Preece, *Minority Rights: Between Diversity
    and Community*, Cambridge: Polity, 2005; also Gad Barzilai,
    Communities and Law: Politics and Cultures of Legal Identities,
    Ann Arbor, MI: University of Michigan Press, 2003.
2   An estimated 25 percent of "Turks" in Germany are members
    of Turkey's Kurdish minority. A militant faction of this
    minority has been waging an insurrection to achieve recogni-
    tion for their distinctive culture and language, and the status
    of a separate cultural community. Members of this diaspora
    in Germany have been accused by the Turkish government
    of financing weapons purchases by the outlawed Workers'
    Party of Kurdistan (PKK). Michael M. Gunter, *Kurds in
    Germany: A Political Dilemma*, Boulder, CO: Westview
    Press, 1990.
3   "Official Recognition of Islam in Germany," *Spiegel Online*,
    April 16, 2007.
4   For a version of this scenario, see Walter Z. Laqueur, *The Last
    Days of Europe*, New York: Thomas Dunne, 2007.
5   The Financial Times/Harris poll, August 2007, reported in *The
    Economist*, September 1–7, 2007, p. 54.
6   James C. Scott, *Weapons of the Weak: Everyday Forms of
    Peasant Resistance*, New Haven, CT: Yale University Press,
    1985.
7   For example, Wing Chung Ng, "Becoming Chinese-Canadian:
    the Genesis of a Cultural Category," in Elizabeth Sinn, *The
    Last Half Century of Chinese Overseas*, Hong Kong: University
    of Hong Kong Press, 1998, pp. 203–16.
8   G. N. Levine, *The Japanese-American Community: A Three
    Generation Study*, New York: Praeger, 1981.
9   Psalm 137.

10 Edna Nahshon, *Yiddish Proletarian Theatre: The Art and Politics of Artef, 1925–1940*, Westport, CT: Greenwood Press, 1998.
11 Gerald G. Nash, *A. P. Giannini and the Bank of America*, Norman, OK: University of Oklahoma Press, 1992. Also "Bank of America: Heritage Center," Wikipedia, 2006.
12 For example, see "The Anti-Defamation League of B'nai B'rith," Wikipedia, 2008.

CHAPTER 5 DIASPORAS AND INTERNATIONAL RELATIONS

1 On the ethnic dimension of international relations, the reader might consult Steven Lobell and Philip Mauceri, *Ethnic Conflict and International Politics*, New York: Palgrave Macmillan, 2004; Paul Smith (ed.), *Ethnic Groups in International Relations*, New York: New York University Press, 1991; and David Wippman (ed.), *International Law and Ethnic Conflict*, Ithaca, NY: Cornell University Press, 1998.
2 This principle has been enshrined in the Charter of the United Nations: "Nothing. . .shall authorize the United Nations to intervene in matters which are essentially within the domestic jurisdiction of any state. . ." (chapter 5, paragraph 7).
3 K. S. Greenberg, "Humanitarianism in the post-colonial era: the history of Médecins sans Frontières," *Concord Review*, vol. 13, 2002, pp. 1–36.
4 Feng Li and Jing Li, *Foreign Investment in China*, New York: St Martin's Press, 1999, pp. 40–6.
5 The General Framework Agreement for Peace in Bosnia and Herzegovina was formally signed in Paris on December 14, 1995.
6 Hongying Wang, *Weak States, Strong Networks: The Institutional Dynamics of Foreign Direct Investment in China*, Oxford: Oxford University Press, 2001.
7 Patrick Jude Haney, *The Cuban Embargo: The Domestic Politics of an American Foreign Policy*, Pittsburgh, PA: University of Pittsburgh Press, 2005.
8 On the contribution of diasporas to the economic development of their erstwhile homelands, see Jennifer Brinkerhoff (ed.), *Diasporas and International Development: Exploring the Potential*, Boulder, CO: Lynne Rienner, 2008.
9 "Open Up: A Special Report on Migration," *The Economist*, January 5, 2008, p. 11.

10 "Korea Advanced Institute of Science and Technology," Wikipedia, 2008.
11 "Expulsion of Asians in Uganda," Wikipedia, 2008.
12 For example: Benedict Brogan, "1600 Young British Muslims under M15 Surveillance for Plotting Terror," *Daily Mail online*, November 10, 2006.

CHAPTER 6 DIASPORAS AND ETHNIC CONFLICT

1 For recent descriptions and analyses of ethnic conflict, see Milton J. Esman, *An Introduction to Ethnic Conflict*, Cambridge: Polity, 2004; and Stefan Wolff, *Ethnic Conflict: A Global Perspective*, Oxford: Oxford University Press, 2006. See also Donald Horowitz, *Ethnic Groups in Conflict*, Berkeley, CA: University of California Press, 1986.
2 Harry Bearak, "Immigrants Fleeing Fury of South African Mobs," *New York Times*, May 23, 2008, p. A10.
3 Brendan O'Duffy, "Radical Atmosphere: Explaining *Jihadist* Radicalization in the UK," *PS: Political Science and Politics*, January 2008, pp. 37–42.
4 "Bangla Influence Taking Assam the Kashmir Way," India Post.com, May 4, 2008.
5 Seth Mydans, "A Growing Source of Fear for Migrants in Malaysia," *New York Times*, December 10, 2007, p. A4.
6 Gabriel Thompson, "Arizona Minutemen Driven Largely by Sense of Insecurity," *New Standard*, April 15, 2005. Reproduced by google.com
7 Seymour J. Mandlebaum, *Boss Tweed's New York*, New York: J. Wiley, 1965.

CHAPTER 7 DIASPORAS AND PUBLIC POLICY

1 Far from disappearing, the UN Population Division has calculated that if Japan is to maintain its present ratio of employed to dependent workers, it will have to admit a million immigrant workers annually until 2050. See Gabriele Vogt, "Guest Workers for Japan," reported in *Japan Focus, Asia-Pacific e-Newsletter*, September 18, 2007.
2 "Open Up: A Special Report on Migration," *The Economist*, January 5, 2008, p. 6.

3 The White Australia policy was enacted into law in 1901. Its purpose was to exclude Asians and maintain Australia as a European society. It was gradually dismantled during the 1960s and repealed in 1975. Australia now admits as immigrants and prospective citizens large numbers of Asians.

4 Tariq Modood, *Multiculturalism: A Civic Idea*, Cambridge, UK: Polity, 2007, chapter 6, "Multicultural Citizenship," pp. 117–55.

5 In February 2006, the publication in a Danish newspaper of a series of 12 cartoons portraying the prophet, Mohammad, in an unfavorable light evoked fury and six nights of violent demonstrations in Denmark by Muslim youth. Attacks on Danish diplomatic posts spread throughout the Muslim world.

6 This dilemma is explored by Will Kymlicka in *Multicultural Odysseys: Navigating the New International Politics of Diversity*, Oxford: Oxford University Press, 2007.

7 On dual citizenship and hybridity, see G. Pascal Zachary, *The Diversity Advantage*, Boulder, CO: Westview Press, 2003, pp. 43–6.

8 On policies toward religious communities, see Modood, *Multiculturalism*, pp. 26–7, 30, 72–80.

9 On citizenship policy and practice in Germany, see Zachary, *The Diversity Advantage*, chapter 5, "Europe as a Mongrel Space," pp. 123–47.

10 Throughout his book, Zachary proclaims and argues the benefits of "mongrelization" to individual countries in a globalizing world, as summarized in his conclusion, "A Mongrel World," pp. 273–7.

CHAPTER 8 PROSPECTS AND OUTCOMES

1 nationalityrooms@pitt.edu

2 Victoria Burnett, "Spain's Many Muslims Face Dearth of Mosques," *New York Times*, March 16, 2008, p. A4.

3 The UN Population Division in 2006 estimated the 2050 global population at 9.2 billion. The US Census Bureau estimate in 2004 was 9.5 billion: *World Population Prospects, 2050*, Washington, 2004. The 1999 figure was 6 billion.

4 ". . .Hispanics acquire English and lose Spanish rapidly

beginning with the second generation, and appear to be no more or less religious or committed to the work ethic than native born Whites. . .At present a traditional pattern of political assimilation appears to prevail. . .With each successive generation, social, economic and emotional ties to Mexico diminish." Jack Citrin, Amy Lerman, Michael Murakami, and Kathryn Pearson, "Testing Huntington: Is Hispanic Immigration a Threat to American Identity?" American Political Science Association, *Perspectives on Politics*, 5(1), March 2007, pp. 31–47.

Bibliography

Al-Haj, Majid, *Immigration and Ethnic Formation in a Deeply Divided Society: The Case of the 1990s Immigration from the Former Soviet Union in Israel*, Leiden, Netherlands: Brill, 2004.

Arudou, Tabito, "Japan's Future as an International Multicultural Society: From Migrants to Immigrants," *Japan Focus: An Asia-Pacific e-Journal*, October 29, 2007.

Ateek, Naim Stifan, *A Palestinian Theology of Liberation*, Maryknoll, NY: Orbis, 1989.

Avineri, Shlomo, *Zionism as a Movement of National Liberation*, Jerusalem: Israel Information Center, c. 1975.

Barzilai, Gad, *Communities and Law: Politics and Culture of Legal Identities*, Ann Arbor, MI: University of Michigan Press, 2003.

Bean, Frank D., de la Garza, Rodolfo O., Roberts, Bryan R., and Weintraub, Sidney, *At the Crossroads: Mexican Migration and US Policy*, Lanham, MD: Rowman and Littlefield, 1997.

Bejarano, Cynthia J., *Que Onda? Urban Youth Culture and Border Identity*, Tucson, AZ: University of Arizona Press, 2005.

Bonacich, Edna, "A Theory of Middleman Minorities," *American Sociological Review*, 1973, pp. 583–94.

Bonacich, Edna and Modell, John, *The Economic Basis of Ethnic Solidarity: A Study of Japanese-Americans*, Berkeley, CA: University of California Press, 1980.

Brah, Avtar, *Cartographies of Diaspora: Contested Identities*, London: Routledge, 1996.

Brand, L. A., *Palestinians in the Arab World*, New York: Columbia University Press, 1988.

Braziel, Jana Evans and Mannur, Anita (eds.), *Theorizing Diaspora: A Reader*, Oxford: Blackwell, 2003.

Brinkerhoff, Jennifer (ed.), *Diasporas and Development: Exploring the Potential*, Boulder, CO: Lynne Rienner, 2008.

Brinkerhoff, Jennifer, *Digital Diasporas: Identity and Transnational Engagement*, New York: Cambridge University Press, forthcoming.

Brogan, Benedict, "1600 Young British Muslims Under M15 Surveillance for Plotting Terror," *Daily Mail online*, November 10, 2006.

Brubaker, Rogers, "The 'Diaspora' Diaspora," *Ethnic and Racial Studies*, 28(1), 2005, pp. 1–19.

Burns, Michael, *France and the Dreyfus Affair: A Documentary History*, Boston, MA: Bedford/St Martin's Press, 1999.

Cafferty, Pastora San Juan and Engstrom, David W. (eds.), *Hispanics in the United States*. New Brunswick, NJ: Transaction, 2000.

Chertoff, Mordecai S., *Zionism: A Basic Reader*, New York: Herzl, 1975.

Chinese Affairs Commission, *Overseas Chinese Economy Yearbook*, Taipeh, 1999.

Christison, Kathleen, *The Wounds of Dispossession: Telling the Palestinian Story*, Santa Fe, NM: Sunlit Hills Press, 2001.

Citrin, Jack, Lerman, Amy, Murakami, Michael and Pearson, Kathryn, "Testing Huntington: Is Hispanic Immigration a Threat to American Identity?" American Political Science Association, *Perspectives on Politics*, 5(1), March 2007, pp. 31–47.

Cohen, Robin, *Global Diasporas: An Introduction*, Seattle, WA: University of Washington Press, 1997.

Cornell, Stephen and Douglas Hartman, *Ethnicity and Race: Making Identities in a Changing World*, Thousand Oaks, CA: Pine Forge Press, 1998.

Coughlin, Richard, *Double Identity: The Chinese in Modern Thailand*, Hong Kong: Hong Kong University Press, 1960.

Crouch, H., *Government and Society in Malaysia*, Ithaca, NY: Cornell University Press, 1996.

Davis, Darien J., *Afro-Brazilians: Time for Recognition*, London: Minority Rights Group International, 1999.

Douglass, Mike and Glenda Susan Roberts (eds.), *Japan and Global*

Migration: Foreign Workers and the Advent of a Multicultural Society, London: Taylor and Francis, 1999.

El Najjar, Hassan A., *The Gulf War: Overreaction and Excessiveness*, Dalton, GA: Amazone Press, 2001.

Esman, Milton J., *Administration and Development in Malaysia*, Ithaca, NY: Cornell University Press, 1974.

Esman, Milton J., *An Introduction to Ethnic Conflict*, Cambridge: Polity, 2004.

Faist, Thomas, "Transnationalization in International Migration: Implications for the Study of Citizenship and Culture," *Ethnic and Racial Studies*, 23(2), 2000, pp. 189–222.

Fuller, Thomas, "Indian Discontent Fuels Malaysia's Rising Tensions," *New York Times*, February 10, 2008, p. A6.

Furnival, J. S., *Colonial Policy and Practice: A Comparative Study of Burma and Netherlands India*, Cambridge: Cambridge University Press, 1948.

Gabaccia, Donna R., *Italy's Many Diasporas*, London: UCL Press, 2000.

Galper, Allan S., *From Bolshoi to Be'er Sheba: Scientists to Streetsweepers: Cultural Dislocation among Soviet Immigrants in Israel*, Lanham, MD: University Press of America, 1995.

Ghabra, Shafeeq N., *Palestinians in Kuwait: The Family and the Politics of Survival*, Boulder, CO: Westview Press, 1987.

Gold, J., *The Israeli Diaspora*, Seattle, WA: University of Washington Press, 2002.

Gomez, Edmund Terence and Jomo, K. S., *Malaysia's Political Economy: Politics, Patronage, and Profits*, Cambridge: Cambridge University Press, 1997.

Gunter, Michael M., *Kurds in Germany: A Political Dilemma*, Boulder, CO: Westview Press, 1990.

Haddad, Yvonne and Balz, Michael J., "The October Riots in France: a Failed Immigration Policy or the Empire Strikes Back," *International Migration*, 44(2), 2006, pp. 25–34.

Hamilton, Charles V., Huntley, Lynn, Alexander, Neville, Guimaraes, Antonio Sergio Alfredo, and James, Wilmot (eds.), *Beyond Racism: Race and Inequality in Brazil, South Africa, and the United States*, Boulder, CO: Lynne Rienner, 2001.

Haney, Patrick Jude, *The Cuban Embargo: The Domestic Politics of an American Foreign Policy*, Pittsburgh, PA: University of Pittsburgh Press, 2005.

Herzl, Theodor, *A Jewish State: An Attempt at a Modern Solution of the Jewish Question*, New York: Federation of American Zionists, 1917 (trans. of *Der Judenstaat*, 1900).

Horowitz, Donald, *Ethnic Groups in Conflict*, Berkeley, CA: University of California Press, 1986.

Horowitz, Tamar (ed.), *Children of Perestroika in Israel*, Lanham, MD: University Press of America, 1999.

Isajiw, Wsevolod, *Understanding Diversity: Ethnicity and Race in the Canadian Context*, Toronto: Thompson Educational, 1999.

Jackson-Preece, Jennifer, *Minority Rights: Between Diversity and Community*, Cambridge: Polity, 2005.

Jerusalem Report, November 26, 2007, 18(16), pp. 13–15.

Khan, Joel S. and Loh Koc Wah (eds.), *Fragmants of Vision: Culture and Politics in Contemporary Malaysia*, Sydney: Allen and Unwin, 1992.

Khouri, Fred, *The Arab–Israeli Dilemma*, Syracuse: Syracuse University Press (3rd edn), 1985.

Kraay, Hendrik (ed.), *Afro-Brazilian Culture and Politics*, New York: M. E. Sharpe, 1998.

Kymlicka, Will, *Multicultural Odysseys: Navigating the New International Order of Diversity*, Oxford: Oxford University Press, 2007.

Lancyk, Ann, *Ukraine and Ukrainians Throughout the World*, Toronto: University of Toronto Press, 1994.

Laqueur, Walter Z., *The Last Days of Europe*, New York: Thomas Dunne, 2007.

Lazear, Edward P., *Mexican Assimilation in the United States*, Stanford, CA: Hoover Institute Press, 2005

Leal, David L., Nuno, Stephen A., Lee, Jongho and de la Garza, Rodolfo, "Latinos, Immigration, and the 2006 Midterm Elections," *PS: Political Science and Politics*, 41(2), pp. 309–17.

Leveau, Arnaud, *Le destin des fils du dragon*, Paris: Le Harmattan, 2003.

Levine, G. N., *The Japanese-American Community: A Three Generation Study*, New York: Praeger, 1981.

Lobell, Steven E. and Philip Mauceri, *Ethnic Conflict and International Politics*, New York: Palgrave Macmillan, 2004.

Lucasson, Leo, *The Immigrant Threat: The Integration of Old and New Migrants into Western Europe since 1850*, Urbana, IL: University of Illinois Press, 2005.

McCaffrey, Lawrence J., *The Irish Diaspora in America*, Bloomington, IN: Indiana University Press, 1976.

Mandelbaum, Seymour J., *Boss Tweed's New York*, New York: J. Wiley, 1965.

Martinez, Oscar J., *Mexican Origin People in the United States*, Tucson, AZ: University of Arizona Press, 2001.

Massey, Douglas S., et al., *Beyond Smoke and Mirrors: Mexican Immigration in an Era of Economic Integration*, New York: Russell Sage Foundation, 2002.

Mauceri, Philip, *Ethnic Conflict and International Politics*, New York: Palgrave Macmillan, 2004.

Modood, Tariq, *Multiculturalism: A Civic Idea*, Cambridge: Polity, 2007.

Mudimbe, V.Y. and Chungmoo Choi, *Diasporas and Immigration*, Durham, NC: Duke University Press, 1997.

Munz, Rainer and Ohliger Rainer (eds), *Diasporas and Ethnic Migrants: Germany, Israel and Post-Soviet Successor States in Comparative Perspective*, London: Frank Cass, 2003.

Nahshon, Edna, *Yiddish Proletarian Theatre: The Art and Politics of Artef, 1925–1940*, Westport, CT: Greenwood Press, 1998.

Nash, Gerald G., *A. P. Giannini and the Bank of America*, Norman, OK: University of Oklahoma Press, 1992.

Ng, Wing Chung, "Becoming Chinese-Canadians: The Genesis of a Cultural Category," in Sinn, Elizabeth (ed.), *The Last Half Century of Chinese Overseas*, Hong Kong: University of Hong Kong Press, 1998, pp. 203–16.

Nga Longva, Anh, *Walls Built on Sand: Migration, Exclusion, and Society in Kuwait*, Boulder, CO: Westview Press, 1997.

"Open Up: a Special Report on Migration," *The Economist*, January 5, 2008.

Portes, Alejandro and Rumbaut, Ruben G., *Legacies: The Story of the Second Generation*, Berkeley, CA: University of California Press, 2001.

Purcell, Victor, *The Chinese in Southeast Asia*, Oxford: Oxford University Press, 1965.

Roland, Edna Maria Santos, "The Economics of Racism: People of African Descent in Brazil," paper presented at the Seminar on the Economics of Racism, Geneva, sponsored by the International Council on Human Rights Policy, November 24–5, 2001.

Refsing, K., "*In* Japan but not *of* Japan," in MacKerras, Colin (ed.), *Ethnicity in Asia*, New York: Routledge Curzon, 2003, pp. 48–63.

Reichmann, Rebecca (ed.), *Race in Contemporary Brazil*, University

Park, PA: Penn State University Press, 1999.

Reid, Anthony (ed.), *Sojourners and Settlers: Histories of Southeast Asia and the Chinese*, Sydney: Allen and Unwin, 1996.

Reis, Michele, "Theorizing Diaspora: Perspectives on Classical and Contemporary Diaspora," *International Migration*, 42(2), 2004, pp. 41–60.

Reische, Diane L., *Arafat and the Palestine Liberation Organization*, New York: F. Watts, 1991.

Safran, William, "Comparing Diasporas: A Review Essay," *Diaspora*, 8(3), 1999, pp. 225–307.

Sakanaka, Hidenori, "The Future of Japan's Immigration Policy," *Japan Focus*, April 15, 2007, trans. by Andrew Taylor and David McNeill.

Sanders, Ronald, *The High Walls of Jerusalem: A History of the Balfour Declaration*, New York: Holt, Rinehart, and Winston, 1984.

Satzewich, Vic, *The Ukrainian Diaspora*, New York: Routledge, 2002.

Scott, James C., *Weapons of the Weak: Everyday Forms of Peasant Resistance*, New Haven, CT: Yale University Press, 1985.

Sheffer, Gabriel (ed.), *Modern Diasporas in International Politics*, London: Croom Helm, 1986.

Sheffer, Gabriel, *Diaspora Politics: At Home Abroad*, New York: Cambridge University Press, 2003.

Sher, Gilead, *The Israeli–Palestinian Peace Negotiations, 1999–2001: Within Reach*, London and New York: Routledge, 2006.

Silverstein, Paul J., *Algeria in France: Transpolitics, Race, and Nation*, Bloomington, IN: Indiana University Press, 2004.

Singh Tatla, Darshan, *The Sikh Diaspora: The Search for Statehood*, Seattle, WA: University of Washington Press, 1999.

Skinner, G. William, *Chinese Society in Thailand: An Analytical History*, Ithaca, NY: Cornell University Press, 1957.

Smith, Paul (ed.), *Ethnic Groups in International Relations*, New York: New York University Press, 1991.

Subtelny, Orest, *Ukraine: A History*, Toronto: University of Toronto Press, 1994.

Supong Chantavanich, "From Siamese-Chinese to Chinese-Thai: Political Conditions and Identity Shifts in Thailand," in Leo Suryadinata (ed.), *Ethnic Chinese as Southeast Asians*, Singapore: Institute of Southeast Asian Studies, 1997, pp. 232–59.

Suryadinata, Leo (ed.), *Ethnic Relations and Nation-Building in*

Southeast Asia: The Case of the Ethnic Chinese, Singapore: Institute of Southeast Asian Studies, 2004.

Telhami, Shibley, *Power and Leadership in International Bargaining: The Path to the Camp David Accords*, New York: Columbia University Press, 1990.

Telles, Edward E., *Race in Another America: The Significance of Skin Color in Brazil*, Princeton, NJ: Princeton University Press, 2004.

Telles, Edward E. and Ortiz, Vilma, *Generations of Exclusion: Mexican-Americans, Assimilation, and Race*, New York: Russell Sage Foundation, 2008.

Tololyan, Khachig, "Rethinking Diasporas: Stateless Power in the Transnational Moment," *Diaspora*, 5(1), 1996, pp. 3–36.

Troper, Harold and Weinfeld, Morton, *Old Wounds: Jews, Ukrainians and the Hunt for Nazi War Criminals in Canada*, Markham, Ontario: Penguin, 1988.

Van Hear, Nicholas, *New Diasporas: The Mass Exodus, Dispersal, and Regrouping of Migrant Communities*, Seattle, WA: University of Washington Press, 1998.

Vatikiotis, Michael, "Thailand: Sino Chic: Suddenly Its Cool to be Chinese," Far *Eastern Economic Review*, January 11, 1996, p. 22.

Vella, Walter F., *Chaiyo! King Vajiravudh and the Development of Thai Nationalism*, Honolulu: East-West Center Press, 1995.

Vertovec, Steven, *The Hindu Diaspora, Comparative Patterns*, New York: Routledge, 2000

Vertovec, Steven and Cohen, Robin, *Migration, Diasporas, and Transnationalism*, Cheltenham, UK: Edward Elgar, 1999.

Vital, David, *The Origins of Zionism*, Oxford: Clarendon Press, 1975.

Vital, David, *Zionism: The Formative Years*, Oxford: Clarendon Press, 1982.

Vital, David, *Zionism: The Crucial Phase*, Oxford: Clarendon Press, 1987

Vogt, Gabriele, "Japan Focus," *Asia-Pacific Newsletter*, September 18, 2007.

Von Vorys, Karl, *Democracy without Consensus: Communalism and Political Stability in Malaysia*, Princeton, NJ: Princeton University Press, 1975.

Wang Gungwu, *The Overseas Chinese*, Cambridge, MA: Harvard University Press, 2000.

Wang Hongying, *Weak States, Strong Networks: The Institutional Dynamics of Foreign Direct Investment in China*, Oxford: Oxford University Press, 2001.

Wertsman, Vladimir, *Ukrainians in America, 1608–1975: A Chronology and Fact Book*, Dobbs Ferry, NY: Oceana Publishers, 1976.

Wihtol de Wenden, Catherine, "Changes in Maghrebi Association Movements," in John Rex and Beatrice Drury (eds.), *Ethnic Mobilization in a Multi-Cultural Europe*, Aldershot, UK: Ashgate, 1994, pp. 106–15.

Winckler, Onn, *Demographic Developments and Population Policies in Kuwait*, Tel Aviv: Moshe Dayan Center for Middle East and African Studies, 1998.

Wippman, David (ed.), *International Law and Ethnic Conflict*, Ithaca, NY: Cornell University Press, 1998.

Wolff, Stefan, *Ethnic Conflict: A Global Perspective*, Oxford: Oxford University Press, 2006.

World Bank, *Migration and Remittances Factbook*, Washington, DC, March 2008.

Wu Yuan Li and Chun-shi Wu, *Economic Development in Southeast Asia: The Chinese Dimension*, Stanford, CA: Hoover Institute Press, 1980.

Zachary, G. Pascal, *The Diversity Advantage*, Boulder, CO: Westview Press, 2003.

Zha, Daojiong, "Chinese Migrant Workers in Japan: Policies, Institutions, and Civil Society," Monterey Institute of International Studies, 2003.

Zuniga, Victor and Hernandez-Leon, Ruben (eds.), *New Destinations: Mexican Immigration in the United States*, New York: Russell Sage Foundation, 2005.

Index